greek and
roman coins

greek and roman coins

James A. Mackay

Arthur Barker Limited
5 Winsley Street London W 1

ISBN 0 213 00350 3

Printed in Great Britain by
C. Tinling & Co. Ltd, London and Prescot

contents

foreword

From the invention of coinage in the early decades of the seventh century BC to the fall of the Western Roman Empire in 476 AD is a period of time spanning eleven hundred years. During this period, particularly in the pre-Christian era, coins were minted in numerous towns, cities and petty states in the civilised world centred on the Mediterranean. It is hardly surprising, therefore, that this aspect of numismatics has been the subject of a vast literature covering every facet of Greek and Roman coins. Of the making of books on Greek and Roman numismatics there seems to be no end and, indeed, the beginner is often deterred from approaching this fertile field on account of the abundance of published material.

In offering this modest contribution to the subject it has been my aim to survey the vast range of classical coins in one volume of convenient size. Inevitably I have not been able to devote as much space as I should have liked to certain aspects of Greek and Roman coins, while others have had to be omitted altogether. I hope, however, that this brief commentary on the development of coinage during its first millennium will help to stimulate further interest in this fascinating field.

If stamps may be said to teach history and geography, the coins of the ancient world may be said to teach not only the history and geography of Greece and Rome but also something of their languages, traditions, folklore and economic patterns. A classical education is not a prerequisite to a study or understanding of these coins, nor is it necessary to have unlimited funds to embark on a collection of Greek or Roman coins. Vast hoards of these coins have been found, and others are still being discovered, so that the basic material for collection and further research is surprisingly plentiful and comparatively cheap. Indeed, it would be true to say that no other antiquities of comparable age could be obtained today at such moderate cost. It is an ironic commentary on our standards of value that a fine Athenian 'owl' may be purchased today for less than some of the more elusive dates of modern British or American coins, whose intrinsic and aesthetic qualities are questionable.

I am indebted to Messrs Christie, Manson and Wood, Messrs Sotheby, Wilkinson and Hodge, and Miss Heather Salter, Editor of *Coins* (Link House Publications) for the illustrations reproduced in this book and to my friend, Colin Narbeth, for his helpful comments and for checking the manuscript. I should also like to thank Mrs J. M. O'Halloran for coping with the manuscript in her usual efficient manner and producing the typescript.

James A. Mackay
Amersham, Bucks
March 1971

1 before coinage

Nowadays coins are mundane objects which we take for granted and it would be hard to imagine a world in which they did not exist. The coins of the modern world, mass-produced base-metal objects, are merely tokens, their value implied by the figures inscribed on them. It is only in our ultra-sophisticated society that (despite a certain amount of protest) people would accept as worth 50 new pence (or 10 old shillings) a piece of metal in size and weight barely larger than the 10 new pence (2 shillings) and somewhat smaller than the now defunct halfcrown – which represented only a quarter of its value.

Although coins in gold were in circulation within living memory, and some silver coins (in Britain, France and the United States among other countries) are still in current use, we have long since ceased to regard these handy bits of metal as representing the value actually stamped on them. Since modern coins, like paper money, have no intrinsic value it follows that they can only be invested with value in a certain clearly defined area where the authority of the government making the issue is recognised. In times when coins were valued on their precious metal content there was a far wider circulation of money irrespective of national boundaries. Good examples of internationally accepted coins were the Spanish 'pieces of eight' and, in more recent times, the Mexican and British Trade Dollars. A modern analogy would be the Maria Theresa dollar of Austria and the British gold sovereign, both of which are highly respected to this day in the countries of the Middle East. Although the image of these coins is important, it is their silver or gold content which establishes their purchasing power.

Long before the emergence of the first circular metal discs which can be dignified by the name of coins, mankind in many parts of the world, in the Mediterranean lands, in western Asia and in the Far East, had progressed to the point where the barter of goods which were surplus to requirements, in return for other goods which were needed, had become unmanageable and it was necessary to substitute for cattle and ox-hides some primitive form of currency which would be readily acceptable by all parties in transactions. The Chinese solved the problem by inventing small bronze pieces which were, in effect, miniature representations of the knives, spades and billhooks which, at an earlier date, had been used for barter in agricultural communities.

A parallel use of articles connected with husbandry is found in Europe during the first millennium BC, in the small bronze celts or axes used for barter in Gaul (now France) and the iron rods or spits used in Greece. These spits have an interesting etymology connected with the origins of numismatics. In the original form the word for a spit or dart was *belos* (our word *bolt* is derived from it). Add the prefix *o-* and we get *obelos* which, in its diminutive form, becomes *obeliskos*. Although the term 'obelisk' is used nowadays for something quite the reverse – a pointed square pillar – in ancient times it meant a small iron spit. The standard unit of barter in Greece was a handful of spits, reckoned to be six of these rods. The word for a handful was *drachma* (from the verb *drassomai*: 'I grasp') and this term came eventually to be transferred to the basic unit of currency in Greece. The word *obelos* in due course became transmuted into *obolos,* a unit of weight equivalent to a sixth of a drachma and hence also a coin of equivalent value. Additionally it is interesting to note that Plutarch uses the word *obeliskos* for a coin stamped with a spit, the significance of which is referred to later.

Another common term from the ancient world which had importance both as a weight and as a symbol of value was the talent, referred to so often in the Bible. In its original form the talent (*talanton*) was an ox-hide. Large pieces of metal (usually bronze) were fashioned into the rough shape of an ox-hide and used in primitive financial transactions. This type of barter currency had its origins in Babylon and spread throughout the countries of the Middle and Near East, including Assyria, Egypt and Greece. If Homer is to be believed the talent in the first millennium BC was of gold, but the weight of the Homeric talent referred to in the *Iliad* is unknown. The Mycenaean culture of prehistoric Greece regarded the talent as a weight of about 60 pounds avoirdupois. In Cyprus, however, where copper has been mined since time immemorial (and gave that island its name), the bronze talent was considerably greater in weight. The talent of Attica (the district in which Athens was the chief town) weighed about 57.75 lb. The talent of silver was divided into 60 *minae* worth 100 drachmae each and was used as the basic unit of weight in bullion transactions throughout the pre-Christian era.

Gold has exercised a peculiar fascination over mankind since prehistoric times. It is apparently found in every language except Maori, the original settlers of New Zealand alone having no use for the stuff, and has been sought after and fought over for countless ages. Inevitably the next stage in moving from bartering in actual commodities, and from thence to the use of bronze or iron substitutes, was the use of bars, ingots and rings made of gold. At what point in the development of civilisation men began trading in precious metal as an elementary form of currency is not known, but this practice was certainly established during the first half of the first millennium BC (i.e. by the eighth century before Christ). There were attempts to establish relationships between the various metals. Gold was reckoned to be the most valuable, one part by weight being worth about thirteen of silver or 3,000 of copper. Another metal which crops up continually in the early history of coinage was electrum, sometimes known as pale gold or white gold, a natural alloy of silver and gold which was usually reckoned as being one tenth as valuable as pure gold.

According to Herodotus, the fifth century BC Athenian historian, the invention of coinage, as distinct from currency, was traditionally credited to the Lydians. Historical and archaeological research in recent years has confirmed this, though the date of the invention is not now regarded as having been as early as was originally thought. Certainly it is true that the peoples of Lydia and the coastal cities of Ionia, in Asia Minor (modern Turkey), were handling small bars or ingots of electrum which bore, by way of identification, a mark or marks applied by merchants and traders. These marks were small rectangular punches applied with a broken nail or spit (that *obeliskos* again). When the spit was broken in two, the jagged end formed an admirable tool for punching ingots. As no two jagged edges would be the same, this expedient was a most effective method of producing a unique mark of identity, readily recognisable by the merchant who stamped it.

These early punch marks on electrum dumps were not struck by royal or civic authority but were merely a guarantee by a merchant of the purity of the piece of metal. The irregularity of the weights of these dumps shows that at this early stage weight was not of primary consideration. The trader was only concerned with making up the metal into a handy-sized lump which he would then sell or exchange for other goods as advantageously as possible. It was therefore necessary to weigh these pieces at every transaction. At a subsequent date, however, the weight of pieces of electrum became gradually more standardised and the punch marks correspondingly more elaborate.

The earliest of these pieces were Lydian staters of the second half of the seventh century BC. The electrum from which they were made was dredged from the river beds of the Tmolus mountains of Anatolia. The stater was a weight, usually equated with the pound and common in Babylonia, Persia and Lydia. The British Museum collection possesses a fine example of these primitive staters, weighting 10·81 grams. The obverse, or 'heads' side, is blank but for slight striation, caused by minute ridges on the anvil on which the molten lump of electrum was placed for striking. These narrow ridge-marks on the obverse have no significance, but indicate that the top of the anvil was purposely roughened so that the electrum could be held in place more easily.

The reverse (or 'tails' side) of this piece bears three small rectangular punch marks, two squares, and an oblong in between. The marks of these incuses seem to indicate some elaborate system of coding or identification and point to a civic, rather than a private, issue. The great numismatic scholar Babelon, in *Les Origines de la Monnaie, 1897*, was of the opinion that the three marks were the 'signatures' of various private merchant-bankers, but a close examination of the marks reveals that they were struck to an equal depth, and must therefore have been applied simultaneously. Probably some sort of trident arrangement was used; two of the marks are typical of the broken nail strikes previously employed, but the middle mark has some semblance of a symbolic design on it (if one uses one's imagination).

The fabric of this early stater is elliptical and bean-shaped, as one would expect from a piece of molten metal held in tongs over an anvil. The incuse marks applied by a trident would have been struck with a hammer which, while producing the force to make the punch marks, would not have hit the metal itself. When coinage did become established and proper reverse dies covered the whole surface of the flan (the technical name for the blank piece of metal), the evenness of the striking resulted in the flattened circular object which is so familiar to us as a coin.

Although the kingdoms of Asia Minor and the countries of the Greek world were quick to adopt coinage from the latter half of the seventh century BC onwards it is curious to note that the Phoenicians and their off-shoot, the Carthaginians) were slow to follow suit; while the Romans who, after the era of the Alexandrian Empire in the fourth and third centuries, became masters of the ancient world, did not begin using coins as such until 269 BC. Prior to that date the Romans had a primitive currency based, like that of the Greeks of prehistory, on bronze. Large, roughly-shaped chunks of bronze, known as *aes rude* (rough bronze) formed the coinage of Rome. Interesting parallels from more recent times are the ponderous copper pieces of medieval China and seventeenth-century Sweden.

2 the archaic period
630–500 BC

Numismatic scholars over the centuries have been accustomed to divide the coinage of the Greeks and their contemporaries into seven periods. The chronological divisions of these periods has altered considerably, even within the past seventy years, and even after the tremendous amount of research which has taken place in Greek numismatics in the past two decades we should not regard the present classifications as final. Although the somewhat arbitrary grouping of the periods may alter from time to time the actual coins in these categories remain unchanged and since the classification was traditionally based on artistic and stylistic grounds the names by which these periods are known are also unchanged.

Until comparatively recently numismatists placed the invention of coinage somewhere at the end of the eighth century BC. The evidence of coin hoards and other archaeological discoveries in recent years, however, have resulted in a reassessment of the early chronology of coins and a rather more modern date, somewhere in the latter half of the seventh century, has been fixed for the earliest coins of Asia Minor. Although considerable controversy has raged over the vexed question of where and when the earliest coins were produced, the consensus of opinion is that the first pieces minted by authority were the electrum staters struck in Lydia in the second half of the seventh century BC. These may have been minted under King Ardys, his son Sadyattes, or even as late as his grandson Alyattes, but somewhere about 630 BC electrum staters were produced with an obverse design showing a

14

lion's head, emblem of the Mermnad dynasty of Lydia. Where this piece differed radically from the electrum dumps of an earlier generation, giving it the definite character of a coin, was in its decorative obverse. Whereas previously it had been sufficient to place the lump of metal on a ridged anvil, the anvil was now engraved intaglio with a deliberate design. When the molten metal was placed on the anvil and struck with a hammer the design on the anvil was transferred to the coin in relief. The reverse, or upper side of the coin flan, bore the incuse mark of the punch with which it was struck.

Apart from the appearance of these coins, the main differences between them and the merchants' bean-shaped dumps was that they bore a regal emblem and this automatically implied that not only the purity, but the weight and thus the value, of the coin was guaranteed within the realms of the issuing authority. The convenience of coins was not lost on the merchants of Asia Minor and the practice of coining money in this way spread rapidly throughout that area and the trading cities of the Aegean coast known as Ionia. In the coastal regions trade was in the hands of Greeks who had colonised the seaboard of Anatolia. From Ionia the vogue for coins spread to the islands of the Aegean and the Mediterranean and eventually to the mainland of Greece.

Though Lydia was the first country to adopt coinage, the Greek seaports of Ionia are probably of greater numismatic importance, partly on account of the number of different mints which were in existence in the earliest period, and partly on account of the great diversity of coin types which they produced. Many of the towns of Ionia, such as Miletus, Abydus and Phocaea, were important commercial centres, so not only were they prolific issuers of coins, but their coins were dispersed in the course of trade all over the Greek world and have turned up in coin hoards often a considerable distance from Asia Minor.

Phocaea is regarded as having been among the first Ionian cities to adopt coinage, the familiar electrum coins bearing the helmeted profile of the warrior goddess Athena dating from the middle of the fifth century BC and alluding to the city's Athenian origins. The earliest coins of Phocaea, however, date from about 600 BC and have a fairly simple obverse showing a seal and a capital letter *theta* (Θ). Two points of interest are raised by this design. The depiction of a seal (in Greek, *phoke*) is a kind of pun and does not allude to the origins of the town, which was traditionally regarded as having been established by settlers from the mainland Greek district of Phocis, led by two Athenians. In its heyday Phocaea was a thalassocracy (maritime power dominating the surrounding coastal area) but after 560 BC its importance gradually waned until it was defeated and conquered by the Persians in 541 BC. The other point about the obverse is the use of the capital letter *theta* instead of *phi* for the initial of Phocaea, illustrating the development of the Greek alphabet at this time.

Phocaea produced coins in electrum and silver and such was its commercial importance that its coins were imitated (as regards weight, at any rate) by several other cities of Ionia, notably Cyzicus on the southern shores of the Black Sea. The electrum used for the coins of Phocaea was remarkably good, being slightly over 50 per cent gold. For the reverse of the early coins two incuse marks were used on the staters and a single punch for the smaller denominations.

Like Phocaea, Chios used coinage of electrum and gold, the earliest coins appearing at the turn of the sixth century. These coins featured the simple emblem of the island, a seated sphinx, and this remained on the Chian money struck right down to the third century AD. The coins minted at Ephesus in the seventh century featured a bee, the symbol of that city. The electrum used for the Ephesian coins was of a comparatively poor quality.

Among the most important cities of Ionia, both politically and economically, at this time was Miletus and its coins began to appear very soon after the kings of Lydia introduced this handy form of currency. The early electrum coins of Miletus are particularly interesting on account of the great variety of obverse types, which were mostly heraldic in character. Animal symbols, such as a stag, a winged bull or lions' heads, were used for the obverse, while various combinations of incuse marks appeared on the reverse. The position of Miletus at the crossroads of the Greek world and the Orient is reflected in the coin types and the artistic styles adopted; winged female deities and semi-human figures such as the winged man-bull testify to Assyrian influence. Although the

16

majority of coins not only of this period but also of the subsequent century bore no inscription at all, or only some rudimentary abbreviation for the issuing authority's name, a notable exception was the electrum stater featuring a stag and bearing (in Greek) the inscription 'I am the badge of Phanes', this otherwise unrecorded individual having been the magistrate during whose period in office the coin was struck. This is the earliest known example of an inscribed coin, and a fairly verbose inscription it was at that.

Coined money spread from Asia Minor to mainland Greece in the latter half of the seventh century BC. Traditionally, credit for the first coins of Greece proper is given to the island of Aegina which was conquered by Pheidon, King of Argos. Even at that early stage Aegina had attained considerable importance as a trading centre and it seems logical that Pheidon should have established his mint there. In the *Etymologicum* of Orion, based on the writings of the fourth century BC historian Heracleides of Pontus, there is a statement that 'Pheidon of Argos first of all men struck coins in Aegina, and having issued coins, he removed the spits and dedicated them to the Argive Hera'. Archaeological excavation at Aegina in the nineteenth century produced some astonishing confirmation of this story. When the temple dedicated to the goddess Hera was excavated the remains of iron spits deposited there in Pheidon's day were unearthed. These *oboloi* had been bound together with iron bands and embedded in a lead foundation. Nearby was found a curiously shaped iron bar of approximately the same weight as the bundle of spits, both being about 400 times the weight of the corresponding amounts in Pheidonian silver coins.

Pheidon produced silver drachmae and obols on what became known as the Aeginetan weight standard. The obverse featured a leather-backed turtle, the badge of Aegina. Turtles of this kind are found to this day in the seas around the island. The reverse had a large incuse mark in the form of a rectangle intersected by diagonal lines like the British flag. The 'turtles' of Aegina were the world's first international coinage and circulated widely all over the Eastern Mediterranean. The appearance of the leather-backed turtle on these coins varies considerably in attention to detail. In some cases a mere outline of the animal's shell was given; but in

17

other cases some attempt was made to show stylised detail (a row of small pellets down the centre) or the individual segments of the shell. Although the basic design of these coins was simple, the die-engravers attained a fairly high degree of skill in reproducing minor details. Even after the collapse of the Pheidonian empire the turtles of Aegina were faithfully minted and remained basically unchanged for almost two hundred years.

Nearby Corinth, at the head of the Saronic Gulf, was quick to emulate the silver coins of Aegina, though a different, slightly heavier weight standard was used. The coins of Corinth depicted the famous winged horse, Pegasus, whom the hero Bellerophon had tamed on the hill of Corinth. Beneath the horse was a tiny Q-shaped letter, the *koppa*, which remained on the Corinthian coinage long after it had passed out of general usage and been superseded in ordinary written Greek by the letter *k*. The coins of Corinth also had their nickname, being known as 'foals' (*poloi*). The reverse of the earliest foals had an elaborate punchmark consisting of four triangles arranged in clockwise fashion. Although the Pegasus design remained a constant feature of the obverse types on Corinthian coins, the incuse marks on the reverse gradually developed into a geometric pattern not unlike a swastika. As well as the stater or tridrachm, Corinth minted drachmae and hemi-drachms, the latter on account of their diminutive size and value showing only the forepart of Pegasus. The coinage of Corinth assumed major importance in the sixth century following the establishment of Corinthian colonies in north-western Greece. The principal colony was Corcyra (Corfu) and from this base in what are now the Ionian Islands the Corinthians spread northwards into modern Albania, establishing colonies at Epidamnus (Durazzo) and Apollonia. The earliest coins used by these colonies were rough parodies of the Corinthian Pegasus types but by the middle of the sixth century distinctive drachmae featuring a cow's head were in circulation and this motif subsequently developed into the representation of a cow suckling a calf (drachmae) and the forepart of a cow (hemi-drachms). More elaborate incuse markings were applied to the reverse of these coins.

At the time that coinage became popular in mainland Greece, Athens was undergoing a period of economic stagnation as a result of her crushing defeat by the Aeginetans in 665 BC. Two generations elapsed before Athenian prosperity, founded on a traditional pottery industry, began to recover. By the beginning of the sixth century Athens was producing dumpy silver coins featuring an amphora (oil or wine vessel) on the obverse and a rectangular incuse mark similar to that found on contemporary Aeginetan turtles. The amphorae depicted on these coins alluded to the manufacture of such vessels at Athens. At a somewhat later date the fabric of Athenian coins was altered to a much thinner, more regular shape, and, at the same time, the style of amphora was changed. The later amphorae, ovoid in shape, were typical of those found on the Tyrrhenian coast of Italy and for some time scholars and numismatists questioned the origin of the coins on these grounds. Archaeological excavation in the past fifty years, however, has revealed vessels of this type in Greece and proved them to be of Athenian manufacture. From archaeological evidence it has been demonstrated that these thinner coins date from about 580 BC.

A curious economic situation occurred in Athens as a result of the introduction of coinage. The bulk of the coined money came into the hands of the wealthy upper class, and the working classes were forced into debt in their attempts to get hold of the new-fangled coins. Ultimately the bulk of the lower classes were reduced to a state of slavery and inevitably this led to revolution. The people overthrew the regime and placed the government in the hands of Solon, whose solution to the problem was the immediate cancellation of debts involving the security of the debtor's person, drastic revision of the constitution and legal system and a reform of the currency. The value of the Athenian drachma was reduced from 70=1 mina to 100=1 mina. The new coins perpetuated the oil vessel and incuse mark designs but were of a reduced size and weight. The denominations in currency were the didrachm (2 drachmae) and obol, coined on what is usually termed the Euboic-Attic standard.

Having reformed the laws and the currency of Athens Solon departed on foreign travel which lasted four years. Shortly after his departure the wealthy family of the Alcmaeonidae returned to Athens from exile and gained control of the state. This was reflected in a new issue of coins superseding the amphora types. The Alcmaeon coins showed the *triskeles* (the three-legs device found on the heraldic badges of Sicily and the Isle of Man), which was the personal emblem of the Alcmaeonidae. From about 590 BC onwards there was a succession of different coin types, bearing the heraldic devices of various leading families in Athenian society. In the Athenian coins in the period from 590 to 566 the Athenian staters and lesser denominations depicted a wheel, a beetle, a bull's head, and parts of a horse's anatomy. It is impossible to assign these types to an exact date within this period of oligarchy (rule by a privileged few), since the various families were continually jostling for power, and it is likely that more than one of these distinctive obverse types was in use at any one time. Somewhere in this period, however, there appeared silver coins of a higher denomination and, for the first time, an attempt was made to provide the reverse with a pictorial design instead of a geometric incuse mark. These larger coins were tetra-drachms (four-drachmae pieces) and they bore the helmeted profile of Athena, patron-goddess of the city, on the obverse and an owl – her emblem – on the reverse. The transition from the purely incuse marking hitherto used is shown by the sunken rectangular frame in which the little owl was set. But the owl itself was depicted in relief, and a further innovation was the inclusion of the letters *AΘE* (*Athe*) an abbreviated form of the city's name.

The famous 'owls' of Athens, destined to enjoy a lengthy existence in many variations over a period of three centuries, were introduced in 566 by Pisistratus who had gradually won ascendancy over his oligarchic rivals in the previous four years. In 566 he instituted the Panathenaean Games to promote the cult of the goddess Athena and it was logical that she should be placed on the coins of the state. During the ensuing decade Pisistratus became even more powerful, and was virtually king of Athens until 576 BC when the oligarchic opposition forced him into exile. Under the oligarchs Athens seems to have dropped the Athena type of coins for a while, reverting to the earlier national emblems and badges of the aristocratic families. Some of these showed a bull's head (symbol of the powerful Eteobutadae clan); others featured the head of a gorgon on one side and an owl on the other. About 546

20

BC, however, Pisistratus made a comeback, landing near Marathon and defeating the oligarchic forces at Pallene. The Alcmaeonidae and their adherents fled into exile once more and from then until his death in 527 BC Pisistratus reigned supreme. In this period the Athena and owl coin types were reintroduced and developed rapidly in execution and design, attaining a high standard of excellence. Curiously, although Athena was engraved in profile her eye was shown as if she were staring straight out of the coin. This odd 'full-face' eye with a 'side-face' portrait was a peculiarity of Greek coins for several generations.

During the reign of Hippias (527–510 BC) the Athena and owl types continued to develop. The owls especially were engraved with great care and some attempt was made to show the feathers in considerable detail. Although the Athena was realistically portrayed, the profile was far too large for the flan and often parts of the design would be off the flan on account of bad centring. This lack of proportion spoiled an otherwise fine coin design. Under Hippias special coins were minted for the Panathenaean Festivals held every four years. In his reign there were four such festivals, between 522 and 510, and coins struck to honour these occasions reverted to the earlier uniface pattern with a symbol (crab, leaf, amphora) on the obverse and an incuse reverse. The Alcmaeonidae, who had settled at Delphi, raised a mercenary army and, aided by Sparta, invaded Athens in 510 BC and drove out Hippias. Electrum coins, struck to pay their troops, bore the emblems which the aristocracy had earlier placed on the coins of Athens – the *triskeles* and bull's-head. These and other old aristocratic types were resurrected on the coins struck under the oligarchy of 510–507 BC. These coins bore an incuse square on the reverse, but within the square was placed in relief a bull's head and later a lion's head. A full-face portrait of a gorgon appeared on the obverse of many of these coins.

In 507 BC Isagoras attempted to seize power with the aid of a Spartan army which, for a time, occupied the Acropolis. The people of Athens, however, rose against the tyrant and besieged the Spartans who subsequently evacuated the citadel, leaving the followers of Isagoras to their fate. Democracy, under the Alcmaeonid Cleisthenes, was restored to Athens. Under

Corinth stater *c.* 330 BC obv: Athena rev: Pegasus

Cleisthenes silver coins in denominations from the tetradrachm to the diminutive half obol were struck with Athena obverse and owl reverse. He also introduced a triobol with a bareheaded Athena on the reverse, and also a coin of half that value (tri-hemi-obol) with a double-headed Athena on the obverse and a helmeted profile of the goddess on the reverse. These smaller denominations indicate a significant change in the use to which money was being put. Hitherto coins had been, in the main, a convenient method by which the wealthier individuals could store their wealth. Now, however, coins were being used as a method of payment for ordinary artisans and labourers and vast quantities of these low denominations were circulated in everyday business and small transactions.

The practice of striking coins with designs on both sides spread from Athens to Corinth about the middle of the sixth century. Corinthian didrachms were produced in a slightly heavier standard than had previously been used, to bring the currency of Corinth into line with the contemporary Athenian standard. The new coins had Pegasus on the obverse as before but the reverse featured the profile of a goddess. The goddess depicted was Athena, adapted to local purposes by the Corinthian style of helmet. On the smaller denominations the bare-headed profile of Aphrodite was substituted.

To the north of Athens lay the large island of Euboea whose most important city, Chalcis, began to coin money in the latter half of the sixth century. At Chalcis the worship of Zeus was well established and it was appropriate that the coins of this city should feature the eagle and serpent which were this god's particular attributes. The reverse of these coins featured an incuse triangle or square containing a wheel and the first three letters of the city's name in Greek lettering. It is curious to note that in Chalcidian practice a symbol closely resembling the Greek letter *psi* (*Ψ*) was used instead of the more usual *chi* (*X*). The coins of Chalcis continued down to 506 BC when the city became a dependency of Athens and Athenian coinage was substituted.

In neighbouring Boeotia the small towns and cities banded themselves together in the mid-sixth century to form the Boeotian League. The most important towns in this confederacy were Thebes, the administrative capital of the League, Tanagra, its principal market town and commercial centre, and Coronea, which had particular religious significance. Coins of the League may have been minted in the first two cities, though it has been deduced from the uniformity of the Boeotian coin types that possibly only one mint was employed. The standard obverse design was a Boeotian shield, symbolising the defensive nature of the League, while a rectangular incuse mark with crossed diagonal lines appeared in the reverse. The earliest coins bore no inscription, but later TT or TA (the abbreviation for Tanagra) was adopted and these tiny monograms may be found in the indentations at the sides of the shield. Finally, although a standard design and uniform fabric were used for the coins of the Boeotian League, it became the custom to insert a letter in the reverse incuse mark to denote a particular city of the League where the coins were intended for circulation. Thus the letters *A* (Aulis), (Pharae), *H* (Haliartus), *O* (Thebes), *M* (Mycalessus) or *Q* (Coronea) may be found. More elaborate inscriptions consisting of BOI (Boeotia) and TA (Tanagra) were placed on coins which are thought to have been intended for circulation throughout League territory, and seem to reinforce the theory that Tanagra was the chief (if not the only) mint for the Boeotian League. The sole exception to this was Orchomenos which refused to join the League with the other Boeotian towns and maintained its monetary independence by minting small coins (obols) featuring an ear of corn and the letter E in the obverse and the popular 'Union Jack' rectangular incuse mark on the reverse.

In the closing decade of the sixth century Boeotia and Euboea formed an alliance with Sparta against Athens. This alliance was alluded to in a series of tetradrachms minted about 510 BC with the Chalcidian wheel on one side and a Boeotian shield on the other. Curiously enough, these coins were struck on the Attic (Athenian) standard, to which Chalcis was reluctantly committed for economic reasons. The link-up of Euboea and Boeotia was emphasised by placing the initial letter *Chi* on the Boeotian shield. The Boeotians reciprocated by minting similar coins (but on the Aeginetan weight standard) with the letters BOI or TA within the wheel of Chalcis. Unfortunately for the allies, Athens concentrated her forces against them and defeated the Boeotians and then the Euboeans in two battles fought on the same day. Chalcis came under Athenian control while the Boeotian League was forced to cede some of its most valuable territory to the victors. As a result Chalcis ceased to mint coins while Tanagra diminished in importance and coins of the League were henceforward produced at Thebes. These coins were distinguished by their motif of a wine-jar (a reference to the god of wine, Dionysus, who was particularly revered at Thales) and the shield of the Itonian Athena.

The Greek cities of the sixth century coined their money in silver since it was the only precious metal available to them in any quantity. On the other side of the Aegean, however, there was a relative abundance of electrum so it was natural that the coinage of Asia Minor should be in the gold-silver alloy. One of the big snags about electrum was that the intrinsic value of the metal could vary considerably according to the proportions of gold to silver in the electrum. One of the most famous kings of all times, whose name is still synonymous with untold wealth, was Croesus, who ascended the throne of Lydia in 564 BC. Like his predecessors, Croesus struck electrum coins, though the heraldic emblem on the obverse was changed. Whereas King Alyattes had depicted two half-lions, Croesus substituted a bull's head for one of these. The reverse bore two incuse marks side by side and the fabric of the coins was bean-shaped as before.

a Persia double-daric *c.* 330 BC obv: King of Persia with bow and arrow;
b Persia daric *c.* 450–400 BC obv: King of Persia

a   b

Croesus was dissatisfied with electrum as a medium for coining money and decided to substitute for it a coin in pure gold. Since gold was generally regarded as about a third more valuable than electrum of the same weight, he reduced the size of his first gold coins to three-quarters that of the electrum staters, so that they would be on par with each other. This paved the way for the withdrawal of electrum altogether and the substitution of pure silver for coins of lower value. The first silver coins were struck on the same weight as the gold staters, but the ratio of gold to silver was about 13·5 to 1. Croesus solved this awkward problem by reducing the weight of his gold staters to three-quarters, so that a gold stater became equivalent to ten silver staters or double shekels. At the same time half units or shekels were minted, 20 silver shekels being equal to a gold stater – a bimetallic system which survived, in the United Kingdom at least, 2,500 years later. Croesus also produced smaller gold coins in divisions of a third, sixth and twelfth of a stater. Croesus came up against the growing might of the Persian empire in the middle of the sixth century and decided to have a showdown with the great king Cyrus. He consulted the oracle at Delphi before embarking on this campaign and was told that his action would destroy an empire. Croesus fell for this ambiguous reply and launched a war with the Persians, resulting in his defeat and the overthrow of his own empire, which was assimilated into the dominions of Cyrus. Sardis, the Lydian capital, became the administrative centre of a Persian satrapy or province.

Prior to this date the Persians had not used coins but henceforward the empire of Cyrus adopted a bimetallic system and established the first Persian mint, probably at Sardis. Though Cyrus imitated Croesus by coining 20 silver pieces to the gold stater he clung to the ancient Babylonian weight standard which was somewhat heavier than the former Lydian standard. These silver coins were known as *sigloi* and at some subsequent date the gold pieces were called darics (*dareikos*, after the Emperor Darius who ascended the throne in 521 BC). Because the gold coins were named after him it became a tradition to credit the introduction of coinage in Persia to Darius, but though he undoubtedly extended the use of coinage to all parts of his dominions it is considered by numismatists and archaeologists that the earliest coins of the Persian empire were the direct successors of the Lydian shekels and staters. These coins featured the Persian ruler himself, the first coins to depict a living person, a practice which was not emulated anywhere else in the ancient world for five centuries. The reverse of these coins bore an oblong incuse mark and the flan of the coins was often, though not always, oval in shape. The darics and sigloi of the Persian Empire won wide acceptance all over the Eastern Mediterranean and found their way as far afield as Italy and Sicily and throughout the Middle East as far as the frontiers of India. The effigy of the bearded archer-king was preserved on the Persic coins for more than two centuries and influenced the design and character of the coins used by many of the kingdoms and states of the Middle East. In this category came the coins minted in Cyprus by Euelthan, king of Salamis, on the Babylonian or Persic weight standard. These coins had a kneeling ram on the obverse and a smooth, blank reverse.

During the latter half of the sixth century there was a migration of Greeks from the western coast of Asia Minor and the Aegean area before the rising menace of Persia. These displaced communities moved *en masse* to the north and west, to the Balkans, the Black Sea coast, to southern Italy, Sicily and even to the southern shores of what is now France. Since they had enjoyed a fairly advanced state of civilisation in Asia Minor they took their ideals, their culture and their socio-economic patterns with them. Not only did they take their coinage to the outer limits of the Greek world but, in many cases, transplanted the coin types as

Mende tetradrachm 500–450 BC   obv: ithyphallic mule   rev: incuse
square

well, though usually with some improvement in design and finish.
The most important of the Thracian colonies was Abdera whose
coins faithfully imitated the griffin designs of Teos whence the
people of Abdera had come. An interesting feature of these coins is
the inclusion, for the first time, of the initials or names of
magistrates and moneyers, often in association with tiny heraldic
symbols related to these officials. Other important towns and
districts of Thrace which produced notable coinage in this period
included Maroneia (depicting horses) and Dicaea (profile of
Hercules). The most intriguing coins of all emanated from the
island of Thasos at the north of the Aegean. During the second
half of the sixth century these Thasian didrachms and drachmae
had for their obverse type the most erotic designs ever to appear
on any coins in any age. They depicted a naked satyr in the act of
raping a protesting nymph. Variations on this theme were popular
on the coins of Thasos for many years and were copied by the
neighbouring tribes of the Thracian mainland.

Farther south lay the hand-shaped peninsula of Chalcidice
whose prosperous cities perished more than two millennia ago and
are all but forgotten today, their distinctive coins being virtually
the only relics of their vanished civilisation. These cities were
colonised from mainland Greece and the influence of the mother
states, both in design and weight-standards, was strong. The most
attractive coins came from the city of Acanthus which struck
tetradrachms on the Euboic standard, with an obverse showing a
ferocious lion attacking a bull. The smaller denominations
featured a bull on his own or the head and shoulders only. Lions
and wild bulls were prevalent in the north-eastern Aegean area in

27

the sixth century BC so these coin types were quite appropriate. The Chalcidicean town of Dicaea also coined money on the Euboic standard, the types closely modelled on those of Eretria in Euboea. The obverse showed a cow in the act of scratching her ear with her hind hoof. Like the coins of Eretria, the Dicaean coins had a reverse design in an incuse rectangle, but whereas the Eretrian coins featured a cuttlefish the Dicaean coins depicted a cock.

Among the earliest of the Chalcidicean cities to coin money was Potidaea whose Euboic tetradrachms portrayed the sea-god Poseidon mounted on horseback (betraying Corinthian influence) with a saltire cross in an incuse square on the reverse, not unlike the contemporary Athenian aristocratic coinage. Terone, famous as a centre of the Thracian wine-producing district, chose a wine jar for the obverse of its tetradrachms. Another of the great centres of viticulture was Mende and it likewise referred to its wine trade on its coins, though somewhat obliquely. The usual obverse of Mendean coins was an ass, an animal closely associated with Dionysus the wine-god who was particularly revered in that district. The technique and usage of coins spread from these Greek colonies to the native tribes of Thrace. Chief among those of Chalcidice were the people of Bottiaea whose capital was the ancient town of Olynthos. The coins of the Bottiaeans had a cow-and-calf motif which scholars have linked with similar emblems found in early Minoan art. To the north-west of Bottiaea lay the native kingdom of Macedon, relatively unimportant in the sixth century but to rise rapidly in the ensuing generations and eventually, in the fourth century BC, to gain mastery of the Greek world. The kings of Macedon did not begin to coin money until the early fifth century.

The Greek colonies which had been established in Sicily and southern Italy in the seventh century BC were not far behind mainland Greece in the introduction of coinage. Among the first of these colonies to use coins was the city of Naxos, which had been colonised by people from the Aegean island of that name. The important feature of the coins of Sicilian Naxos was their obverse and reverse designs. Within a few years of the first Athenian owls Naxos became the second city to produce coins with a design on both sides, favouring a profile of Dionysus and a bunch of grapes respectively. Next in chronological order comes the northern town of Himera whose didrachms featured a cock and an incuse reverse. This device was intended as a pun on the name of the town, the Greek word *hemera* meaning 'day' or 'day-break', associated with the cock-crow. Selinus, deriving its name from the wild celery (*selinon*) which grew in the banks of its river, adopted a celery leaf for its coins. Acragas (Agrigentum) minted Attic-standard didrachms depicting an eagle and a river crab.

The most important of all the Sicilian colonies was Syracuse, which also minted coins on the Attic standard (not so much out of loyalty to the mother-state, Athens, as because it corresponded conveniently with the local Sicilian weight system). At the time of the introduction of coinage to Syracuse the city was ruled by the Gamorvi, or landed oligarchs, whose emblem was a racing chariot drawn by four horses. Chariots, horsemen or chariot wheels were therefore apt symbols for the design of the coins ranging in value from tetradrachm (20 Sicilian litrae) down to the humble obol (sixth of a drachma). The only exception to this theme was the litra (a fifth of a drachma) which had a profile of Arethusa on the obverse and a cuttlefish on the reverse, alluding to the maritime importance of Syracuse. These coins all had interesting reverse types, the larger denominations featuring Arethusa surrounded by dolphins. The drachma omitted the dolphins with Arethusa promoted to the obverse side. The values of the larger coins were cunningly referred to by the number of horses depicted. Thus a quadriga, or four-horse chariot, appeared on the tetradrachm, a man holding two horses on the didrachm, and a man on horseback on the drachma.

Towards the end of the sixth century coinage appeared in Leontini and Gela, both influenced to some extent by Syracuse, with which they were allied. The tetradrachms of Leontini bore a quadriga, closely resembling the Syracusan design. Indeed, E. Boehringer, in his monograph on the coinage of Syracuse, had shown that on at least one occasion Leontini borrowed a quadriga coin die from Syracuse. The reverse of the Leontini coins was a pun on the name and showed a lion's head surrounded by ears of corn. Gela also favoured the chariot motif for the obverse of its

a Agrigentum didrachm 6th century BC obv: eagle rev: crab; *b* Syracuse tetradrachm 478–467 BC obv: quadriga rev: female and dolphins

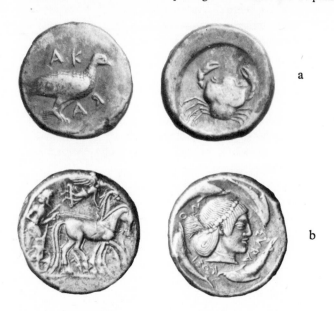

a

b

coins, but depicted the monstrous river-god Galas, a man-headed bull, after whom the city was named.

Across the Straits of Messina were the rich Greek colonies of Magna Graecia (Latin for Greater Greece). Despite their close ties not only with their Sicilian neighbours but with the mother-states of Athens and Corinth, these cities, with the exception of Hyele and Cumae, produced highly distinctive coins which had no parallel in any other part of the Greek world. Although they adhered to Greek weight standards these coins were struck on very thin flans, using obverse and reverse dies which corresponded in such a way that the same motif appeared on both sides, but in relief on the obverse and intaglio on the reverse. Scholars have puzzled over the method by which these coins were struck with such precision that the dies always fitted neatly. Some means of hingeing the dies must have been evolved in order that they should always have corresponded so closely. Another important feature of these coins

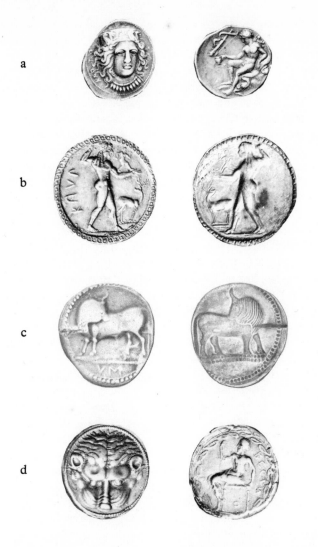

a Croton stater *c.* 420–390 BC obv: Hera Lakinia rev: Herakles; *b* Caulonia stater *c.* 550–480 BC obv: figure of Apollo rev: same, but incuse; *c* Sybaris stater *c.* 560–510 BC obv: bull rev: same design incuse; *d* Rhegium tetradrachm *c.* 460 BC obv: Lion rev: bearded man, seated was the circular frame of cabled border on the obverse, not designed purely for ornament but to impart strength to the flan and prevent it from cracking under the stress of striking or in subsequent handling when such a thin fabric might otherwise have become damaged. Charles Seltman has advanced the plausible theory that one man was responsible for these innovations – someone who had mastered the techniques of fine engraving, who had a keen artistic sensibility, who understood certain engineering principles and who had a mathematical bent which turned his interest to contemporary financial problems. In particular the techniques of the 'lost-wax' process, from which the principle of pressure-moulded ridges shown in the cabled border was borrowed, seem to point to someone with Samian connections, since it was via the craftsmen of Samos that the Greeks acquired this knowledge from Egypt about 550 BC. The one person who neatly fits this description is Pythagoras, the famous mathematician, philosopher and metal-worker of Samos, who migrated to Croton in Magna Graecia about 535 BC, at the time when these coins are thought to have first appeared. The coins of Croton featured a large tripod and were struck on a wide flan in this curious relief and intaglio manner. Subsequently this fashion spread to Caulonia (Apollo and Kaulos-twig), Metapontum (ear of barley), Sybaris and Pyxus (backward-glancing bull), Poseidonia (Poseidon), Tarentum (Apollo and lyre or Phalanthus riding on a dolphin), Rhegium (human-faced bull) and Zancle (dolphin in a sickle-shaped harbour).

At Hyele, otherwise known as Elea or Velia, Greeks from Ionia had founded a colony some time after 544 BC, following the Persian invasion of the Aegean coastal districts of Asia Minor. The earliest coins were similar to those minted by the Greek colony of Massilia (now Marseilles) in the mid-sixth century showing a lion gnawing a bone. The Massilian Greeks had also come originally from Ionia and were in many respects akin to the people who settled at Hyele. At a later date the Eleans continued to use a lion motif, but it became increasingly stylised as first-hand memory of what this animal looked like receded. Although the most northerly city of Magna Graecia, Cumae, was traditionally regarded as the earliest of the Greek colonies of southern Italy, it was the last to adopt a system of coinage. No coins of note were produced in Cumae until the beginning of the fifth century.

Finally, in this survey of Greek coinage of the earliest period, down to the end of the sixth century, some mention must be made of the Greek colonies in North Africa. The earliest of the Greek trading posts in the dominions of the Pharaoh of Egypt was at Naucratis but the coins handled there were those of Miletus or Aegina. Farther west, the Greek colony of Cyrene in what is now Libya rose to importance in the sixth century on account of its export of silphium, a plant used extensively in spices and drugs in ancient times. About the middle of the century Cyrene began coining silver tetradrachms, didrachms and drachmae depicting the silphium plant or parts of it, such as its seeds, the stalk or the leaf. The reverse was an incuse mark not unlike that on contemporary coins of Rhodes, while the weight standard adopted was Euboic, reflecting the cosmopolitanism of Cyrene and the many disparate influences of other Greek districts upon it.

3 the transitional period 500–404 BC

By 500 BC the practice of striking coins had spread throughout the Greek world and extended to many parts of the Mediterranean and the Middle East. The fabric of these coins was fairly uniform in character: a design in varying degrees of elaborateness on the obverse and, as a rule, some sort of incuse marking on the reverse. At the beginning of the fifth century BC the obverse designs were simple in concept, being usually confined to basic heraldic devices, such as the turtle of Aegina or the winged horse of Corinth, but greater attention was now being paid to the detail and finish of the engraving. There is no clear-cut dividing line between the Archaic period and the Transitional period in Greek numismatic art, though for the sake of convenience 500 BC is as good a date to choose as any. It comes mid-way between the first incursions of the Persians into Europe in 512 BC and their crushing defeat at Marathon in 480 BC. Darius I secured a foothold in Europe when he persuaded the ruler of Macedon to accept Persian overlordship. More significant numismatically, the Persian empire annexed the rich silver-bearing district of Thrace.

The chief political event at the beginning of the fifth century was the revolt of the Greek district of Ionia, on the western coast of Asia Minor, against Persian rule. Although Athens and Eretria were the only cities of mainland Greece to send actual assistance to the Ionian rebels, the revolt encouraged other districts to throw off their allegiance to Persia. Principal among them was the Thracian Chersonese whose ruler Miltiades (of Athenian descent) struck coins indicating his sympathies with Ionia. The chief town in the Chersonese, Cardia, had been founded by colonists from the Ionian city of Miletus and appropriately the lion of Miletus was featured on the coins of Miltiades. On the reverse appeared the profile of Athena Promachos, patron goddess of the city championing the Ionian cause. These coins were similar in weight to the Attic tetradrachms. Whether Miltiades gave more active support to the Ionians is conjectural, but the fact that the Persians later expelled him from the Chersonese seems to indicate that his sympathies took a practical form.

At Miletus, headquarters of the Ionian revolt, the traditional electrum coinage was revived in place of the Persic gold and silver coins. A wide variety of types appeared on these electrum staters, featuring an eagle, a backward-glancing bull, a galloping horse, a sphinx, a winged horse, a winged bear, a sow and a cock. There has been some speculation regarding coins portraying Athena – thought to have been struck as a mark of gratitude for Athenian aid in general, or, perhaps, to commemorate the arrival of the squadron of twenty Athenian ships which greatly strengthened the Ionian battle fleet.

The Ionian revolt lasted six years before the last shreds of resistance were subdued by the Persians. Two years later, in 491 BC, Thrace and Macedon were brought back under Persian control. At the same time Darius was able to extend his rule into the north of Greece proper by annexing the northern part of Thessaly. In this period appeared the first coins of Larissa, the most important city of Thessaly, and these conformed to the Persic standard in weight. The drachma featured the sandal which Jason lost while crossing the river Anaurus on his way to Ioleus from Mount Pelion to claim the kingdom from his uncle Pelias, while the hemidrachm portrayed Jason himself, leader of the Argonauts in their quest for the fabled Golden Fleece.

At the same time the Greek islands of the Cyclades, at the southern end of the Aegean, ceased to strike distinctive coins as the Persian naval forces gradually extended their sway across the sea from Ionia towards mainland Greece. The coins of the Cyclades form an interesting group on account of their reverse incuse marks which followed a standard cruciform pattern. The obverse types featured a lyre (Delos), a goat (Paros), a bunch of grapes (Tenos) and a beetle-shaped boat known as a cantharus (Naxos). Although the fabric of these Cycladean coins was similar it is interesting to note that whereas Delos coined on the Attic-Euboic standard, the other three islands clung to the Pheidonian weight system. The independence of the Cyclades, both political and numismatic, came to an end in 490 BC. Both Naxos and Tenos were forced to contribute warships to the Persian battle fleet a decade later though they seized the first opportunity to go over to the Athenian side. Delos and Paros seem to have collaborated more readily with the Persians.

During the year 490 the Persians gradually encroached on the Greek heartland. First the northern Cyclades, then the towns and cities of Euboea, were taken over. Eretria fell after a brief but desperate resistance; the city was razed to the ground and its surviving inhabitants deported to Ardericca near the mouth of the Euphrates in what is now Iraq. The Persians crossed over to the Greek mainland, landing their army at Marathon, twenty-four miles north-east of Athens. Here the might of Darius received its first serious set-back. Although the battle of Marathon was by no means decisive the Athenians and their Plataean allies defeated a numerically superior force and boosted Greek morale enormously. It was in recognition of this victory that the Athenians added three or four olive leaves to the Attic helmet of Athena on their tetradrachms, and there they remained for more than 250 years. The reverse design of the coins was also subtly altered by the inclusion of a waning moon, an allusion to the fact that it was at that time of the month that the battle was fought. This was possibly intended also as a dig at the Spartans, age-old rivals of Athens, whose contingent of troops could not leave their home territory till after the full moon and thus (deliberately or otherwise) arrived at Marathon too late to take part in the fighting.

Little is known of the political situation in the decade between Marathon and the final show-down between East and West which took place at Thermopylae and Salamis, other than that Athens was for part of that time engaged in a war with the neighbouring island of Aegina. Far more important economically, however, was the discovery of large silver deposits at Laurium, on Athenian

a and *b* Athens tetradrachms *c*. 490–430 BC obv: Athena rev: owl

a

b

territory. At first the Athenian government made use of this silver to dole out allowances to its citizens, until Themistocles persuaded the authorities to build a battle fleet of 200 triremes instead. It has been estimated that some 30,000 Athenian citizens received a dole of ten drachmae annually from the excess revenue of the Laurium silver mines prior to the proposal of Themistocles in 483 BC. It was for the purpose of paying this dole that two new denominations were introduced – a decadrachm (enabling the payment to be made literally in a lump sum) and a didrachm which, with two tetradrachms, made up the requisite amount. The obverses of these coins portrayed Athena in much the same way as the tetradrachms, but the owls on the reverse sides differed considerably. That on the decadrachm appeared full-face with wings spread, while the bird on the didrachm was depicted in a rectangular frame. When the dole ceased these denominations were withdrawn.

To the south-west of Athens the city-states of the Peloponnese used the tetradrachms of Aegina as their common currency and medium of exchange. The 'turtles' of Aegina, like the 'owls' of Athens, were popular far beyond the frontiers of the state which coined them. The various towns and cities of the Peloponnese also produced their own local coinage in smaller denominations, mainly obols, hemidrachms and drachmae with distinctive obverse types and incuse reverses, usually containing the initial of the name of the issuing city. Thus coins with the Greek letters A, Σ or M in an incuse square emanated from Argos, Sicyon and Mantinea respectively. Rather more elaborate was the two- or three-letter incuse inscription used by Heraea. The obverse types of these four states were a wolf's head, a dove, a she-bear and a profile of the goddess Hera.

The most interesting of the Peloponnese coins, however, came from Olympia in the territory of Elis. Olympia assumed an importance far beyond its size and commercial status, on account of its association with the pan-Hellenic cult of Zeus. To Olympia came people from all over the Greek world to take part in the four-yearly Olympic Games, to worship Zeus and to spend their money at the great fair connected with the Games. From about 520 BC onwards the Olympic hierarchy coined money in connection with the four-yearly festival. The didrachms, drachmae and smaller denominations depicted an eagle and a thunderbolt, the attributes of Zeus. At the beginning of the fifth century special coins began to be minted at Heraea for the use of the Arcadian Confederation. This political union had its origins in the Arcadian Games, a more local festival than the Olympics but likewise derived from the worship of Zeus. It is curious to note that the dissimilarities of the Heraean coins in a sense complement the Olympic issues: only triobols (hemidrachms) and obols were struck and, instead of merely depicting the symbols of Zeus, the god himself was portrayed, on his throne with eagle and thunderbolt. The reverse types were more elaborate, showing the bust of Despoina (literally 'the Mistress'), daughter of Poseidon and Demeter, whom the Arcadians especially revered. In addition the word *Arkadiqon* (sometimes in abbreviated form) was inscribed on the reverse.

One other issue of a quasi-religious nature remains to be noted in this period. At Delphi in the territory of Phocis, north-west of Athens, was the famous oracle whose pronouncements (as noted in the previous chapter) were often dangerously ambiguous. Despite this the oracle continued to attract a great number of visitors from all over the Greek world and although it never enjoyed the great seasonal influxes of Olympia and Heraea its religious importance sometimes necessitated special issues of coins. Such an issue, for example, was produced about 479 BC to convert into coin the munificent gifts of bullion deposited at the Delphic shrine by the various Greek states in token of their gratitude at divine deliverance from the threat of Persian invasion the previous year. These coins featured a ram's head and a dolphin on the obverse and a highly elaborate geometric pattern incuse on the reverse. In denominations of two and three drachmae, they were larger than those normally struck at Delphi.

While the people of Greece were engaged in the struggle against the Persians their colonies in Magna Graecia (Great Greece, i.e. Sicily and southern Italy) were pre-occupied with the Carthaginians, allies of the Persians who created diversionary attacks to prevent the colonies from sending aid to the motherland. In many ways Sicily can be likened to America in relation to Britain of the seventeenth and eighteenth centuries. For the Greeks of the sixth century BC it was certainly a case of 'Go West, young man'. Thousands left Greece to settle in the rich and fertile island and within a hundred years the cities of Sicily rivalled those of the mother country in size and prosperity. Syracuse, Metapontum, Croton, Zancle, Messana and Sybaris were among the wealthiest towns of the Greek world (the last-named is immortalised in the adjective 'sybaritic' – a synonym for luxurious).

The effect of the Persian Wars was first felt in Sicily in 494 BC when refugees from Samos arrived at Zancle following the collapse of the Ionian revolt. These refugees plotted with Anaxilas, tyrant of Rhegium on the Italian side of the Straits of Messina, and seized control of Zancle whose coins, for the ensuing five years, were produced on the Attic standard with obverse types strongly reminiscent of Ionia – the bull's head, the galley-prow and the lion's scalp. Anaxilas later turned against his Samian allies and seized Zancle whose coins, from about 489 BC onwards, followed the same pattern as those of Rhegium – a lion's head (obverse) and a calf's profile (reverse). It is interesting to note that the calf on the coins of Rhegium and Messene (as Zancle was now renamed) alluded to the rich pastures of the Rhegium district. This area was known, in the Oscan language, as Vitelia (from *vitulus*, a calf) and in a slightly corrupted form came to be used for the whole of the peninsula – Italia.

For the Greeks of Sicily, as for their compatriots at home, 480 BC was a memorable and victorious year. The major rulers of the island, Anaxilas and Gelon of Syracuse, patched up their differences and turned to meet the threat from Carthage whose expedition, led by Hasdrubal, invaded the island in 480 BC. At Himera on the northern coast of Sicily Gelon inflicted a resounding defeat on the Carthaginians who not only surrendered their war-chests but had to pay a ransom of 2,000 talents. According to Diodorus Siculus the Carthaginians offered a golden crown to Demarete, consort of Gelon. This crown weighed a hundred talents, and from it Demarete minted ten-drachmae coins, known as Demareteion after her. Diodorus got his facts slightly confused, since no gold coins were struck. Gelon, however, instituted annual sporting events, known as the Demareteian Games in honour of his wife and in memory of the victory, and as prizes silver decadrachms and tetradrachms were produced with a victorious quadriga on the obverse and the profile of a goddess (variously described as Artemis or Arethusa) on the reverse. This profile was also used for the obverse of an obol struck about the same time. Similar tetradrachms were minted under the authority of Gelon at Leontini. Some of these coins portrayed Apollo instead of his sister Artemis, but otherwise they were similar to the Syracusan pieces in many respects. These Sicilian coins bore inscriptions in a curious mixture of the Greek and Roman alphabets which reflect the dual influences on the cultural and educational development of Magna Graecia.

Two years before the clash between the Carthaginians and the Siciliote Greeks, Theron, tyrant of Akragas, seized Himera and was thus intimately involved in the great battle of 480 BC. The coins of Himera at the beginning of the fifth century had been uniface and showed a cock. The people of Himera decided to strike coins with distinctive types on both sides and, appropriately, placed a hen on the reverse. After Theron gained control of the town the crab, emblem of Akragas, replaced the hen on the reverse of Himera's coins.

With the defeat of Persia in 480 Athens emerged not only as the moral saviour and champion of the Greek world but as the ruling state of Greece in a very real sense. A period of reconstruction was necessary after the war, however, before Athens recovered economically from the strain of the campaign and made good the damage effected by the Persian invasion of Attica. Thus it was that the first new coins of Athens did not appear till 478 BC. The same types were used as before, but subtle modifications, particularly in the details of Athena's hair, were made to the designs. In the period from 478 to 430 BC Athens coined a wide range of denominations, all featuring Athena on the obverse but differing in the reverse designs in several respects. On the tetradrachm, for example, an olive twig and a waning moon were featured beside the owl. On the drachma, obol and hemi-obol the moon was omitted. The triobol or hemidrachm showed a full-face owl between two olive branches, the diobol (third of a drachma) showed two owls face-to-face with an olive spray between them, while the trihemiobol (quarter drachma) showed a full-face owl with wings spread. The Athenian coins of this period were minted in vast quantities and circulated widely all over the ancient world, turning up in coin hoards as far afield as Tunisia, Sicily, Egypt and West Pakistan.

In the years that followed the Persian Wars, Athens extended her sway over the neighbouring cities and petty states. At first these territories were permitted to continue minting their own coins but had to change from local weight systems to the Attic standard. In this category come Thasos, Abdera, Acanthus and the Aegean island of Cos. Gradually, however, Athens won control over coin production in every part of Greece which came under her dominion, and distinctive coins ceased to appear in the territories already mentioned. As Athens extended her authority over other states, they also were forced to give up separate issues of coins. One by one Eretria, Troezen and Aegina ceased to

Lesbos electrum ⅙ stater *c*. 440-350 BC obv: Apollo rev: chariot

produce their own coins and had to accept those of Athens exclusively. In the middle of the fifth century Athens gained ascendancy over the Delian League (established by the Aegean Islands for their mutual protection against primarily Persian aggression) and transferred its treasury to the mainland. In 415 BC Athens went so far as to forbid the striking of non-Athenian coins anywhere in her dominions, which by that time extended from Thrace and the Hellespont to the west coast of Asia Minor and the Aegean Islands. Not only was the minting of silver coins and the use of non-Attic weights expressly forbidden, but people were ordered to hand over what money they had and exchange these coins for Athenian currency.

Curiously enough, this prohibition on indigenous currency did not extend to coinage in other metals and several important commercial centres of the Athenian empire continued to produce coins in gold or electrum. Of these the most important was Cyzicus which struck electrum staters in vast quantities. One Cyzicene stater was on par with 24 Athenian silver drachmae or one Persian gold daric. Apart from the staters there were tetradrachms (sixths) and didrachms (twelfths) in this metal. Although the tunny-fish, civic badge of Cyzicus, appeared somewhere in the design of these coins, the main subject was frequently changed. The coinage of Cyzicus in this period was eclectic, drawing on the coins of other states for artistic inspiration, but naturally Athenian history and folklore provided much of the subject matter.

Phocaea minted large numbers of electrum coins, mostly tetradrachms, showing the familiar seal device, a relic from the earliest period of its coinage. Lesbos, or rather its principal city, Mytilene, favoured coins with a design on both sides, whereas the other Ionian mints retained the incuse square on the reverse. Some of these designs, showing a lion's head or a profile of Hercules, were struck intaglio. Others featured Hermes in an incuse square. A few electrum coins were also minted by the Ionian territories of Chios and Lampsacus.

An indication of the stability and prosperity of Athens at the height of her supremacy in the fifth century is the relative monotony of its coins: their very sameness was a guarantee of continuing public confidence in them (compare this with the use of Austrian Maria Theresa thalers dated 1780, in the Middle East up to the present day). It meant, however, that artists and die engravers could find little scope for their talents in Athens, and in some cases they looked elsewhere for work. Marked Athenian influence is evident in the coins of the Athenian colonies of Amphipolis and Thurii.

Amphipolis, founded in 437 BC, was not permitted to strike coins while it was an Athenian dependency, but thirteen years later, with Spartan aid, it threw off the Athenian yoke and after 424 BC began minting tetradrachms and drachmae, coined from the rich silver deposits of the Mount Pangaeum district. These coins had a type on both sides, a three-quarter face portrait of Apollo on the obverse and a flaming torch on the reverse with the inscription 'of the Amphipolitans'.

Thurii, formerly known as New Sybaris, was jointly founded by Athenians and refugees from the Magna Graecia city of Sybaris after it was sacked by its neighbour Croton in 510 BC. The Sybarites were 'displaced persons' for two generations, and it was not until 455 BC that they settled at Thurii with Athenian assistance. The coins of Thurii are particularly interesting in that they borrowed major types from Athens (Athena) and Sybaris (bull) and modified them to suit their own wishes. Thus the bull of Sybaris, always depicted on Sybarite coins looking back over its shoulder, was now depicted with his head lowered to charge. The anatomical detail shown in these bulls is astonishingly accurate and, incidentally, teaches the veterinary scientist a great deal regarding the evolution of cattle over the past 2,500 years. Athena on the obverse is even more interesting from the technical and artistic point of view. Over the years the profile was developed. The helmet in particular, beginning with a straightforward embellishment of olive leaves, became more and more ornate, until it was elaborately decorated with sea-monsters of various kinds. Another feature of the Thurian Athena was the eye, now rendered realistically instead of in the previous tradition of facing outwards. The coins of Thurii enjoyed a well-deserved reputation in Magna Graecia and the Athena profile was emulated by other cities, notably Neapolis (Naples), Heraclea and Velia. That the engravers were held in high esteem is shown by the inclusion of their names, Histor or Molossos, in the exergue of some of these Thurian coins. (The exergue is a segment of a coin divided by the rest of the field by a line, for instance, the space on an old British penny where the date is shown.)

After Athens defeated Aegina in 456 BC the only serious economic rival to Athens was Corinth whose famous 'foals' continued to appear during the fifth century. The basic types of Pegasus and Athena, established a century earlier, remained the same but as techniques of die-engraving improved and artistic sensibility developed there were subtle changes in these coins. In the early part of the fifth century, about 480 BC, Corinth began striking identical coins for use in her colonies, the sole distinguishing feature being the initial letter of the colony under the horse's belly: alpha (Ambracia), lambda (Leucas) and digamma (Aractorium). (A digamma is an archaic Greek letter like a capital F which had passed out of usage in classical times. The obsolete name of the town in question would have been Faractorium.) Subsequently these colonies opened their own mints and produced local versions of Corinthian foals. The Corinthian coins of this century demonstrate the development of Greek art at this time. The earliest profiles of Athena continue the facing-eye idiosyncrasy but later designs used a more naturalistic approach.

While the coinage of mainland Greece in the fifth century provided little that was completely new and consisted mainly of the development of existing types, a greater variety of types was evident in the coinage of Sicily and Magna Graecia in the same period. Tarentum, one of the most powerful and prosperous of the Greek cities in southern Italy at this time, continued to coin silver staters showing Phalanthus riding on a dolphin, with either a wheel or a profile of Taras, founder of the city, on the reverse. At a later date the profile of Taras was superseded by a seated male figure, leaning forward and holding out a struggling bird to a cat who leaps up to seize it. In both style and subject-matter this unusual reverse betrays the influence of contemporary Athenian art and anticipates the coins of the third century discussed in Chapter 5. Gradually the seated figure reverse was replaced by a figure on horseback – a subject destined to have a long and prolific life. The famous 'horsemen' of Tarentum, as these coins are popularly known, circulated all over Magna Graecia and into other parts of Italy and were the most widely used coins of the peninsula right down to the end of the third century when Roman coins began to oust them. Numerous variations on the horseman type have been recorded: either a man or a boy rider, on horseback, striding beside his mount, or in the act of dismounting. Artistically and technically these silver coins were of a very high order. Although the horseman motif underwent numerous changes, the dolphin obverse remained much the same throughout the currency of these coins.

At the beginning of the fifth century Metapontum abandoned the incuse reverse and produced coins with the ear of barley emblem of the city on the obverse and portrayed various deities and heroes on the reverse: Apollo, Hercules or Achelöos, the river-god. As the century progressed these portraits were transferred to the obverse and the series expanded to include, as well as the afore-mentioned personages, the female deities Hera, Persephone, Athena, Homonoia, Hygeia, Nike and Soteria (allegories of Concord, Health, Victory and Security). Dionysus, Zeus and Demeter were also featured at one time or another, and also a couple of local demi-gods, Leukippos and Tharragoras, who would otherwise be unremembered. In the range and graphic qualities of their portraiture the coins of Metapontum in this period were unrivalled.

Croton also gave up the incuse reverse type in favour of coins with subjects on both sides but the earliest of these coins were content to show the same subject, a tripod, on both obverse and reverse, the only variations being provided by the tiny symbols depicted alongside. Subsequently Hercules, legendary founder of the city, was depicted on the obverse. The reverse, however, presented an odd picture of Apollo and a python flanking a tripod. No doubt the intention of this design was to pay tribute to the sun-god and show him hunting the snake, but the composition of the scene was ludicrous and ill-balanced and the resulting reverse has a curiously whimsical air about it, not found on any other Greek coins. Undoubtedly the artist had been over-ambitious in attempting this composition, but it remains an interesting commentary on the development of Western Greek art in the transitional phase.

With the resumption of democratic government at Rhegium in 461 BC the subjects of its coins were changed from the hare and mule-cart motifs of the tyrant Anaxilas, to a lion's head obverse and a seated figure reverse. This figure has been conjecturally labelled as Lokastos, the mythical founder of the city. Near Rhegium was Croton's colony of Terina which produced some exceptionally beautiful coins in the fifth century. The subject of these coins was a local version of the goddess of victory, profiled on the obverse and depicted as a full-length figure on the reverse. A new series appeared about 420 with Nike depicted in various poses. The Nike of Terina shown on these coins closely resembles the figures of Victory which appeared in the temple of Athena-Nike at the entrance to the Acropolis and it has been supposed that Athenian artists were responsible for the Terina coin-dies. In the north the city of Cumae produced a number of distinctive coin types in the fifth century. A mussel-shell formed the standard reverse of these coins right down to 423 BC when Cumae was captured by the Samnites. The obverse designs began with a lion's scalp flanked by boars' heads but from about 474 BC, when Cumae was allied to Syracuse against the encroachments of the Etruscans, the coin types became more diverse in design, with such subjects as the profiles of goddesses or nymphs.

Just as victory over Carthage in 480 BC had inspired a handsome issue of coins in Syracuse, so also the victory of that city over the Etruscans in 474 BC resulted in a fresh minting of distinctive coins. The naval victory of Syracuse and Cumae over the Etruscans was celebrated by coins showing a chariot with a sea-serpent in the exergue. This reptile symbolised the sea-power of Etruria, now vanquished. The reverse designs of this series featured various female profiles, variations on the theme of the nymph Arethusa. The coins of Syracuse, more than any other Greek state of this century, attained a high standard of excellence in execution, as well as in design. There is ample evidence that coin engraving was regarded in Syracuse as a major art form and during the last third of the century and the early decades of the fourth century this was demonstrated by the inclusion of the names of the designers prominently featured. Among the artists whose names have come down to posterity in this way were Sosion, Eumenos, Eukleidas and Euainetos. Each of these artists excelled his predecessors in turn. Eukleidas produced an elaborate profile of Arethusa adorned with the symbols of Athena, to symbolise Syracusan defeat of the Athenians in 415 BC. But credit for producing the finest coins in this period is due to Euainetos whose magnificent decadrachms appeared after 413 BC and have seldom been equalled, far less excelled, for their technical excellence and artistic brilliance. These larger coins, on account of their size and beauty, have long been regarded very highly by art-connoisseurs and numismatic scholars. Although not particularly rare, such is the demand for these handsome pieces that they now rank among the more expensive coins.

History repeated itself with Syracuse. Just as victory over the Carthaginians had resulted in the Demareteian Games and a special issue of coins, so also the defeat of Athena at Assinarus in 413 BC resulted in the annual festival of the Assinarian Games. It is thought that the prizes awarded at these Games consisted of the weapons and armour taken from the defeated Athenians. Subsequently the prizes were commuted into cash payments for which special coins were struck. These decadrachms bore a four-horse chariot on the reverse with, in the exergue, examples of the Athenian arms and armour labelled *AΘ* (prizes). For the obverse of the coins Euainetos chose a splendid profile of Arethusa, surrounded by dolphins. It is not difficult to imagine with what enthusiasm this magnificent profile was greeted by the Greek

a Syracuse tetradrachm *c.* 412–400 BC obv: quadriga rev: Arethusa and dolphins; *b* Syracuse decadrachm *c.* 412–406 BC obv: quadriga rev: Arethusa and dolphins; *c* Syracuse tetradrachm *c.* 400–387 BC obv: quadriga rev: Arethusa and dolphins

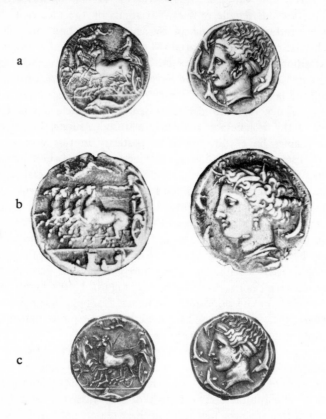

world of the late fourth and fifth centuries. It has been recorded on pottery of southern Italy and was blatantly plagiarised on coins of other territories, as far afield as Spain, Gaul and Italy. In our own time it has been adapted to the postage stamps of both Greece and Italy and currently graces the Italian 500 lire banknote. *La Siracusa,* as the Italians of today call her, has a timeless beauty which no Liberty or Britannia could hope to rival. The Assinarian Games and the large coins which commemorated them combined *a* Naxos tetradrachm *c.* 450 BC obv: Head of Dionysus rev: Silenus and wine cup; *b* Athens *c.* 430 BC obv: Athena rev: owl and names of magistrates; *c* Istrus drachma *c.* 400 BC obv: two male heads, tête-bêche rev: sea eagle on a dolphin; *d* Tenedos drachm *c.* 450–387 BC obv: male and female Janiform heads rev: double axe and grapes

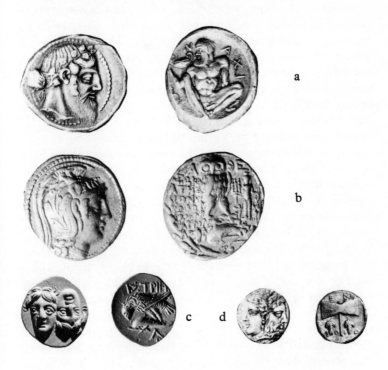

to promote the image of Syracuse in the ancient world. It is hardly surprising, therefore, that the Arethusa decadrachms were minted in large quantities for more than thirty years. Second only to the great master Euainetos himself was his brilliant pupil Kimon, also renowned for his Assinarian decadrachms but probably more famous for his tetradrachms with a facing portrait of Arethusa. Both Euainetos and Kimon were responsible for engraving the dies for gold coins during the siege of Syracuse by the Carthaginians in 400 BC. The reverse designs appropriately

49

showed Hercules throttling a lion, symbolising the life-and-death struggle of the Greeks against the leading African power.

The most important city of Sicily from a numismatic point of view, other than Syracuse, was Catana. Its inhabitants were driven out by the Syracusans in 475 BC and the city was then colonised by its conquerors who changed its name to Aetna. Coins bearing this name first appeared about four years later and consisted of tetradrachms portraying a satyr on the obverse and Zeus on the reverse. In 461 BC the original inhabitants returned to the town and expelled the interlopers. This event is reflected in the coins inscribed KATANE from that date onward, the original name having been re-adopted. New coin types were introduced, featuring the local river-god Amenanos, a man-headed bull, on the obverse and a figure of Victory on the reverse. The amazing quality of perspective shown by the skilful use of engraving, as it were, in layers of background, marks these coins as the work of an outstanding craftsman. The same characteristic is present in the coins of the neighbouring town of Naxos which also regained its independence in 461 BC. The coins of this town featured the profile of Dionysus on the obverse while the reverse showed a satyr drinking wine. These exquisite types continued in use till about 415 BC when Naxos adopted the Syracusan chariot motif, with a full-face portrait of Apollo on the reverse. Other cities whose coinage was remarkably fine in this period were Messana (female deity and Zeus) and Acragas (eagle devouring a hare, and various types of marine life). Much of the coinage of Sicily came to an end abruptly in 410 BC as a result of the Carthaginian invasion which took place in that year. This was a period of temporary coinage in gold, minted by Gela, Acragas and Kamarina, as at Syracuse. These cities, like many others in Sicily, were destroyed by the Carthaginians.

Athens also produced a temporary gold issue about this time, an expedient required by a shortage of silver due to the disastrous Sicilian expedition of 413 BC. Discontent with the high-handedness of Athens had been brewing in the Athenian empire since 432 BC when war against Sparta broke out. The so-called Peloponnesian War dragged on for a whole generation and saw Athens eventually deserted by her allies and her colonies. Even the silver-miners of Laurium, on whose slave labour the empire had flourished, had taken refuge with the enemies of Athens. By 407 BC all the reserves of coined silver had vanished and the once mighty empire was forced to issue tetradrachms and drachmae in copper thinly disguised with a silver wash. The *coup de grâce* was administered in September 405, when the Athenian battle fleet was annihilated at Aegospotami by the combined naval forces of Corinth and Aegina, aided and abetted by Sparta. The collapse of the Athenian empire seemed total at the time, yet such was the resilience of this city-state that it was to recover something of its pristine glory within a decade. Economically and financially, however, Aegospotami marked the end of an era in Greek numismatics.

4 the finest art period
404-336 BC

With the Carthaginian invasion of Sicily and the downfall of
Athens, the last decade of the fifth century saw important political
and economic upheavals which had their inevitable effect on the
coinage of the ancient world. Only in the Peloponnese, whose
states emerged victorious in 404 BC, was there any continuity in
coinage. Under Peloponnesian protection, the independence of
Aegina was restored to her people, but this once great naval power
never recovered its former importance. Symbolic of this loss of
maritime influence was the change in the coinage of Aegina, a
land tortoise being substituted for the sea-turtle as the badge of
the island. Aegina was one of the last states of the Greek world to
produce uniface coins, the 'tortoises' of the fourth century having
an incuse reverse. The dearth of Aeginetan turtles in the fifth
century, after the island became an Athenian dependency, was felt
in the Peloponnese, and in order to relieve the shortage of coinage
in that area Sicyon and Olympia began to strike coins of their own
in varying quantities. Even after the resumption of coinage from
Aegina these states continued to mint their own coins and the
'tortoises' never enjoyed the status which the 'turtles' had had.

Sicyon began minting didrachms about 420 BC, portraying the
chimaera on the obverse and a laureated dove on the reverse.
About the same time there was a revival in the festival coinage of
Olympia and mints were operated at the temples of Zeus and
Hera. The didrachms of this period bore exquisitely engraved
portraits of these divinities. The Zeus temple coinage also included

didrachms featuring a magnificent eagle. That the engravers of these coins were appreciated in their own time is borne out by the inclusion of their monograms; only one has been identified (Polykaon) and the others, whose names began with DA or L, are unknown to posterity.

The supremacy of the Peloponnesian states, under the leadership of Sparta, was short-lived. The Athenian admiral Conon survived the disaster of Aegospotami to avenge himself on the Peloponnesian fleet which he annihilated in 394 BC while commanding the navy of Persia (whither he had taken refuge a decade earlier). As a result of this naval victory at Cnidus the Greek cities on the seaboard of Asia Minor banded together to form a Maritime League. Little would be known of this League were it not for the coins struck by the eight cities of Rhodes, Iasus, Cnidus, Byzantium, Cyzicus, Ephesus, Samos and Lampsacus. With the exception of the last-named, which struck gold staters, these cities minted silver coins with a common obverse type showing the infant Hercules strangling serpents. This device was borrowed from the contemporary coinage of Thebes which was now rising rapidly in importance as a counter to the power of Sparta. The reverse of the League coins featured the civic emblem of the respective cities – the rose (Rhodes), Apollo (Iasus), Aphrodite (Cnidus), a bee (Ephesus), a bull (Byzantium), a tunny-fish and lion's head (Cyzicus) and a lion's scalp (Samos). These coins also bore the letters ΣYN (the abbreviation for the Greek word for 'alliance'). The odd man out, Lampsacus, omitted this abbreviation on its reverse type which featured the forequarters of Pegasus.

The use of a Theban obverse on these coins was a reference to the formation of an alliance with Thebes and Athens in 395 BC against Sparta and as this alliance turned out to be successful in battle many other states joined in. This, in turn, is reflected in the coins of states as far west as Zacynthus and even Croton in Magna Graecia, both of which featured the infant Hercules motif. The alliance received a setback in 387 BC when Sparta ousted Thebes from the leadership of the Boeotian League. As a result the cities of Boeotia began coining their own money again. More for the sake of convenience than to indicate political unity, these towns reclaimed the Boeotian shield for their obverse types but civic emblems appeared on the reverse: a horse (Orchomenos), Poseidon (Haliartus), Hera (Plataea), a horse's fore-parts (Tanagra) and Aphrodite (Thespiae). This coinage was relatively short-lived for Thebes re-asserted her control over Boeotia by about 378 BC and under the brilliant statesman and general, Epaminondas, Thebes was for a time the leading state in Greece. A new federal coinage with a shield obverse and wine-jar reverse came into use. Thebes reached the zenith of her power in 371 BC when Epaminondas defeated the Spartans at Leuctra.

Out of the shattered remnants of the Peloponnese there arose an Arcadian League with its headquarters at the new town of Megalopolis (Great City) founded in 370 BC. Coins for use by the League were produced at Megalopolis showing Zeus and Pan, god of music. A few towns in Arcadia, such as Mantinea, Tegea, Pheneus and Stymphalus, produced attractive didrachms, drachmae and obols of their own featuring local deities. To counterbalance the Arcadian League Epaminondas rebuilt the city of Messene and heavily fortified it. The coins of Messene from 369 BC onwards featured the profile of Demeter and a figure of Zeus on obverse and reverse respectively. Epaminondas next created the Achaean League, with its headquarters at Aegium, in 367 BC. Although this league proved to be ephemeral it is recorded for posterity by the didrachms showing a female profile (thought to be Artemis Laphria) on the obverse and a seated figure of Zeus Amarios of Aegium on the reverse.

The brief period of Theban hegemony did not outlast the death of Epaminondas in 364 BC. By that time Athens had long since recovered from the defeat of 404 and once more occupied a position of paramount importance, though other states were beginning to challenge this position. In the north-east the powerful Chalcidian League, under the leadership of Olynthus, controlled the northern Aegean. The coins of the League portrayed Apollo; both gold and silver were struck in the third decade of the fourth century. The enmity of Sparta undermined the authority of the Chalcidian League. In 379 it was temporarily disbanded and although it was subsequently reconstructed it never regained its former predominance. As the Chalcidian League declined, the neighbouring kingdom of Macedon, which had hitherto been relatively unimportant, began to develop under its dynamic young ruler, Philip II. He imitated the Chalcidians, borrowing the best of their financial and economic structure in building up his kingdom. He struck tetradrachms on the Thracian standard, with a profile of Zeus on the obverse and a horseman on the reverse. The Greek inscription 'of Philip' appeared on the reverse and it was implied that the horseman represented Philip himself. Two years after he came to the throne in 359 BC Philip initiated the policy of expansion which was to take his son and successor as far as the Indian Ocean and North Africa. Philip captured Amphipolis in 357 and Crenides the following year. Macedonians settled in the latter town, which was renamed Philippi. Nearby was Mount Pangaeum, site of the richest gold deposits in the Greek world. The people of Crenides had minted gold staters portraying Hercules and Philip continued the practice, producing the famous staters known as *philippeioi* from 348 BC when he finally over-threw Olynthus. These handsome coins featured Apollo and a *biga* (two-horse chariot) on obverse and reverse respectively. The *philippeioi* captured the imagination of Greece as a whole and they circulated widely all over the ancient world and were even copied by the barbarian Celtic tribes of Western Europe and the Teutonic peoples of the north. Many of these barbarous copies were vigorous if crudely executed; others were but a bare travesty of the Macedonian coins, with no more than a vague suggestion of the Apollo and chariot motifs.

In the ensuing decade Philip consolidated his power in northern Greece, biding his time for an onslaught on the Greek heartland. His opportunity came in 339 BC when war broke out between Amphissa and Delphi. Philip took the part of the latter and invaded central Greece. By championing Delphi Philip gained control of the quasi-religious Amphictyonic Council whose funds he succeeded in appropriating shortly afterwards. From this period date the silver didrachms of the Amphictyons (literally 'the neighbours', the league of Greek states which met at Delphi and Anthela). These coins featured Demeter the corn-goddess on the obverse and a seated Apollo on the reverse. The final confronta-tion between Philip and the Greek city-states came at the battle of

a Macedon Philip II 359–336 BC tetradrachm obv: Zeus rev: horseman;
b Gaul drachma fourth century BC obv: Artemis rev: lion; *c* Larissa
didrachm *c*. 400–344 BC obv: nymph Larissa rev: bridled horse; *d*
Locris, Locri Opuntii stater 369–338 BC obv: Persephone rev: Ajax; *e*
Egypt stater 359–343 BC obv: galloping horse

Chaeronea in 338 BC. Athens and Thebes bore the brunt of the attack while the Peleponnesian states remained aloof, but the defeat of the leading powers in central Greece spelled disaster for Greece as a whole. Seven years later, at the battle of Megalopolis, the Peloponnesian army was annihilated and Macedon became master of the Greek world, from the Balkans to the Mediterranean.

Philip died in 336 and was succeeded by his twenty-year-old son, Alexander, who, by a mixture of statesmanship, diplomacy and ruthlessness, conciliated the former city-states and directed their energies towards a war against Persia. At first Alexander was content to control Greece through a confederation which allowed a certain amount of local autonomy. Alexander's spirit of compromise was reflected in his gold staters which portrayed Athena on the obverse and the figure of Victory on the reverse. This figure was shown with naval insignia, alluding to the Athenian fleet which Alexander employed in his Aegean campaigns. The silver coins struck in Greece under Alexander's authority featured Hercules and Zeus, who were not only revered throughout Greece but had their counterparts in other parts of the ancient world – the Melqart of Phoenicia, Baal of Tarsus, Gilgamesh and Bel-Marduk of Babylon. Gradually also, Alexander rationalised the various weight standards in use throughout the ancient world and introduced uniformity by adopting the Attic standard for the whole of his empire.

5 alexander and his successors 336-30 BC

By the time of his death in 323 BC, at the early age of 33, Alexander had not only conquered Greece and Persia but extended the boundaries of his empire along the coast of North Africa, south through Egypt into Nubia, across Arabia to the Indian Ocean, and in Asia as far as the Punjab. Had he not been stricken by fever at Babylon there is no telling where his ambition would have ended. As it was, the decade of his reign witnessed not only the most rapid conquests of the ancient world but also stupendous efforts of administration and organisation to weld the heterogeneous elements of the empire into a single entity. This is reflected in the coinage of the Alexandrian Empire.

In place of the countless mints which existed in every one of the petty states Alexander established twenty imperial mints. At the same time he strove to achieve uniformity in the coinage used throughout his vast dominions. For the stater and double stater in gold, Athena and Victory were featured on obverse and reverse, while the silver tetradrachm and its subdivisions usually depicted Hercules and Zeus on the respective sides. Some deviation from these types is apparent in the coins produced at certain eastern mints where the god Baal and his attribute, the lion, were shown instead. If the main types were confined to a small range, the scope of these coins was nevertheless enormous. Numerous minor variations are noted in the dies used for the coins of Alexander, while mint marks and the symbols of the magistrates and moneyers add considerably to the variety of the coins. It has been estimated, for example, that the mint of Amphipolis (admittedly the most prolific and active in the empire) employed more than 700 obverse dies and 1300 reverse dies in an eighteen-year period alone. This compares with some 280 obverse and 340 reverse dies recorded as having been used at Syracuse in a period of 140 years. From this astonishing variety of dies it has been deduced that Amphipolis must have produced about thirteen million coins, an astonishing output.

Apart from Amphipolis, which was close to the gold and silver mines of Thrace, the other Greek mints were at Pella, the ancient capital of Macedon, and Sicyon in the Peloponnese, established after Alexander defeated Sparta in 331 BC. In Asia Minor, following Alexander's successful campaign of 334 BC against Persia, Macedonian mints were established at Lampsacus. Subsequently mints were opened at Sardis, Miletus, Caria, Side, Lycia and Pamphylia. In 333 BC Alexander invaded Cilicia and the mint at Tarsus began coining Alexandrian tetradrachms within days of the last Persian staters. Indeed the figure of Zeus on the reverse of the tetradrachms was suspiciously similar to the seated figure of Baal Tars, the local deity hitherto portrayed, an eagle being substituted for a bunch of grapes in the hand of the god. Shortly afterwards Alexander conquered Syria and established a mint at the seaport of Myriandros which he renamed Alexandria (now known as Alexandretta or Iskenderum). A second Syrian mint existed at Damascus. Cyprus, hitherto dominated by the Persian Empire, threw in its lot with Alexander in 332 BC. Salamis, Citium, Paphos and Amathus minted Alexandrian silver tetradrachms from then onwards. Simultaneously four cities of Phoenicia – Sidon, Akka, Aradus and Byblos – began issuing coins for Alexander. At the end of that momentous year Alexander passed into Egypt where he founded the great seaport which still bears his name. Though Alexandria eventually became an important Hellenistic mint it was not until 326 BC that coin production could commence.

At Gaugamela in July 331 BC Alexander defeated the Persians and captured Mesopotamia (modern Iraq), subsequently receiving the surrender of Babylon which was to become, next to Amphipolis, the most important of the Alexandrian mints, employing some 170 obverse and 500 reverse dies in the space of thirteen years. By seizing the rich Persian treasuries at Susa and Persepolis Alexander secured ample bullion to strike gold staters and silver tetradrachms and this explains, in some measure, why the Babylon mint was so prolific. These Babylonian coins bore the mintmark M (for Metropolis), signifying the importance of this city as the centre of the Alexandrian Empire. Shortly before Alexander's death in 323 BC silver decadrachms were struck at Babylon, either with the usual Hercules-Zeus types (for the payment of debts incurred by his forces in the previous campaigns) or with distinctly commemorative types alluding to the battle of the Jhelum river. These handsome coins depicted a horseman (Alexander) attacking an Indian potentate on an elephant – a reference to Rajah Porus who employed a regiment of elephants in the battle. The reverse portrayed Alexander himself, holding the thunderbolt of Zeus in his hand and implying that he was recognised as a god in his own lifetime.

Alexander's untimely death in 323 BC threw his aides into confusion. The ambitious generals who had risen to prominence in his wake elected not one, but two, kings to the throne, the epileptic half-brother of Alexander (Philip III) and the posthumously-born son of Alexander (Alexander IV). With a madman and an infant in the supreme position the generals were enabled to dismember the empire to their own advantage. In the generations which followed the death of Alexander the generals carved out for themselves the great Hellenistic kingdoms of Macedonia, Syria, Egypt, Thrace and Parthia and the Seleucid empire which embraced much of the former Persian dominions. At first these rulers maintained the fiction of a united Alexandrian empire, issuing coins in the names of Philip III and Alexander IV and perpetuating the Hercules-Zeus types of Alexander's reign. Even the free cities on the fringes of the Alexandrian empire minted coins of similar type (though distinguishable from the Alexandrian coins by the comparative thinness and width of the flans).

In 317 BC Olympias, mother of Alexander the Great, murdered Philip, the illegitimate offspring of her late husband Philip II. Seven years later Alexander IV was put to death by Cassander, son of Alexander's general, Antipater. Although the empire was now

Macedon tetradrachm 306–283 BC of Demetrius Poliorcetes obv: prow
of galley rev: Poseidon

without any legal ruler the *de facto* rulers continued to use
Alexandrian coin types, and Cassander even continued, from the
Macedonian mint at Pella, to strike tetradrachms of a type minted
by Philip II. These coins circulated among the Balkan and
Danubian tribes who, like the Arabs and the Ethiopians of a later
age, were very conservative in their partiality to archaic coins.

In the last decade of the fourth century the removal of
Alexander IV had a disruptive effect on the empire. Antigonus and
Ptolemy, ex-generals now ruling Asia Minor and Egypt respectively, actually declared war on each other. Following the defeat
of Ptolemy's navy by Demetrius Poliorcetes, son of Antigonus, in
306 BC both Antigonus and Demetrius assumed the title of
Basileus (king) and the others – Ptolemy, Cassander of Macedon,
Lysimachus of Thrace and Seleucus of Babylonia – were not slow
in conferring royal titles on themselves also. Although they tended
to place their own names on their coins they all exhibited a
remarkable fidelity to the memory of Alexander by retaining the
Hercules-Zeus types. The first major change in coins was made by
Lysimachus who, in fact, substituted for Hercules a profile of the
deified Alexander, with the horn of Jupiter Ammon sprouting
from his temple. This splendid profile ranks as one of the finest
portraits ever to grace a Greek coin. The reverse of these
tetradrachms, minted in Ionia, featured the seated figure of
Athena placing a wreath on the initial letter of Lysimachus – an
allegorical composition which was rather weak, and something of
an anticlimax after the brilliance of the obverse.

At Ipsus in 301 BC Antigonus was killed in battle by the

61

combined forces of the other four Alexandrian generals and his son, Demetrius, was deprived of his kingdom, though paradoxically he retained naval mastery of the eastern Mediterranean, with a strong battle fleet based on Cyprus. Demetrius struck tetradrachms at Salamis featuring victory on the prow of a ship (obverse) and the sea-god Poseidon (reverse). Within four years of Cassander's death in 298 BC, however, Demetrius had secured the throne of Macedon and from about 292 BC the mints at Amphipolis and Pella began producing tetradrachms bearing his profile, perhaps the first occasion in European numismatics that a living person had appeared on a coin (though this custom was fairly common on Asiatic coins from the time of Darius). The cities of Thebes, Demetrias and Chalcis also struck coins in the name of Demetrius, including some gold staters with Alexandrian types. His son Antigonus became king of Macedon in 277 BC after decisively defeating the Gaulish invasion of the Balkans. The coins struck in his name commemorated his victory over Gaul, with the great god Pan on the obverse and Athena on the reverse. Pan was believed to have stricken terror (*panic*) into the hearts of the enemy and caused their rout. Although the profile has all the usual attributes of Pan the features were suspiciously like those of Antigonus. After defeating Ptolemy II of Egypt in 258 by a great naval victory near the Aegean Island of Cos, Antigonus issued new tetradrachms featuring Poseidon and Apollo on obverse and reverse respectively. As well as these distinctive pieces, however, Antigonus continued to mint coins with the Hercules-Zeus types of Alexander. Such coins were favoured during the reigns of Antigonus's successors and it was not, in fact, till 201 BC that the Antigonid ruler Philip V minted silver tetradrachms bearing his own portrait on the obverse and a figure of Athena on the reverse.

Philip was defeated by the Romans at Cynoscephalae in 197 BC. Ironically, gold staters were struck the following year with the haughty profile of the Roman Consul, Titus Quinctius Flaminius, substituted for the portrait of the defeated king. Although Rome continued to exercise suzerainty over Macedon, Philip was permitted some degree of autonomy. This proved irksome and in 186 BC he revolted against Rome, recommencing coinage at Amphipolis and Pella to pay for the campaign. He struck tetra-

Macedon tetradrachm 178–168 BC obv: King Perseus rev: eagle on thunderbolt

drachms (shield and wreathed club), didrachms and drachmae (diademed profile and wreathed club of Hercules). The final confrontation with Rome came in 168 BC when Perseus, son of Philip V, was captured by the Romans after the disastrous battle of Pydna. Henceforward Macedon was divided into four Roman *regiones*. Coins inscribed in Greek 'First' or 'Second' (region) of Macedon were struck at Amphipolis and Salonika respectively, with the profile of Artemis substituted for that of the erstwhile Antigonid rulers. Philip VI of Macedon, thought to have been an illegitimate son of Perseus, attempted a rebellion against Rome in 149. His short-lived revolt is remembered by the coins bearing his beardless profile.

Probably the greatest of the successor states of the Alexandrian empire, at least in geographical area, was that founded by Seleucus the Conqueror, satrap of Babylon, though it was not until 312 BC that his kingdom was established. The Seleucid empire extended from the Aegean Sea to the frontiers of India. The principal cities of this empire were Seleucia on the river Tigris and Antioch in Syria, though, for a time, the main source of his coins continued to be Babylon.

The earliest Seleucid coins followed the Alexandrian pattern though an anchor, emblem of Seleucus, was incorporated on the reverse. The Hercules-Zeus designs were retained for most of the coins struck by Seleucus and his son Antiochus I although there were a number of special issues, particularly the beautiful tetradrachms thought to have been produced at Pergamum in Asia

Minor at the beginning of the third century. These coins featured a war-elephant and a horned horse – the latter being an allusion to Alexander's famous steed Bucephalus (Bull-head). Antiochus I became co-ruler in 293, administering the eastern provinces with Seleucia as his capital. He struck tetradrachms and drachmae with a portrait of Zeus (obverse) and Athena in a war-chariot drawn by elephants.

Twelve years later, when Antiochus I became sole king, the coins of this empire were standardised, with his profile on the obverse and the seated figure of various deities on the reverse (Apollo, Hercules or Zeus). Coins of these types were continued in the reign of his son Antiochus II, but about 246 BC his grandson Seleucus II used a standing figure of Apollo for the reverse. Seleucus III (226–223 BC) reverted to the seated Apollo type. Under Antiochus III, brother of the preceding ruler, a valiant but abortive attempt was made to regain the provinces of the Seleucid empire which had seceded – India, Bactria, Parthia and Pergamum. The campaigns which were fought at the end of the third century were reflected in a revival of elephant coin-types. Seleucus IV (187–175 BC) stuck to the portrait and Apollo designs, as did his successor, his younger brother, Antiochus IV who ruled as joint king with the infant son of Seleucus (known as the baby Antiochus). Coins bore the profiles of either uncle or nephew until the death of the latter in 169 BC. Antiochus IV seized his opportunity to invade Egypt and occupy most of that country down to 164 BC when he died suddenly. During the last five years of his reign Zeus replaced Apollo on his silver coins, while bronze coins, similar to those used in Egypt at this time, were struck on his behalf at Antioch. In 162 BC Demetrius I, son of Seleucus IV, seized the throne and campaigned vigorously for the return of the lost Babylonian provinces. His coins featured a seated figure of Tyche, goddess of good fortune, on the reverse and his portrait on the obverse. An interesting feature of his coins was their dates, reckoned from the beginning of the Seleucid Era in 312 BC.

Demetrius I was eliminated in 150 by Ptolemy VII of Egypt who placed his own nominee, Alexander Balas, on the Seleucid throne. Alexander lasted only four years before being ousted by

Ptolemy. From then until 64 BC, when the Romans suppressed the Seleucid kingdom, there was a profusion of kings in rapid succession, resulting in some interesting variation in coin types – the Heavenly Twins (Castor and Pollux) and Tryphon (144–142 BC), the conjoined profiles of Cleopatra Thea and her son Antiochus VIII (122–120 BC) and the handsome portrait of the Armenian king Tigranes who ruled Syria from 83 to 69 BC. Though the Roman general Lucullus restored the Seleucid Antiochus XIII in 69 BC the country became a Roman province in 64 BC when Pompey the Great annexed it directly.

One of the most remarkable of the Hellenistic kingdoms to emerge in the generations after Alexander's death was Bactria in what is now the Punjab of India. Initially Bactria was a province of the Seleucid empire but by 250 BC its governor, Diodotus, was strong enough to break away from the overlordship of Antiochus II. Numismatically, however, Diodotus preserved the links with the Seleucid empire by retaining the coin types of Antiochus, though substituting his own name. His successor Euthydemus reintroduced a reverse design (hitherto used by the early Seleucids) showing the seated figure of Hercules. What marks the coins of Bactria as outstanding, however, was the magnificence and liveliness of the portraiture on the obverse. The profile of the elderly Euthydemus is too realistic to be flattering but was engraved with such sensitivity as to rank as one of the finest coin portraits of all time. An equally high standard of artistry and technical finish was maintained in the portraits of Demetrius and Antimachus, the later Bactrian rulers.

Under Demetrius I Bactria expanded as far as the frontiers of China and regained the territories of the Indus valley. His coins minted for use in Bactria depicted an elephant head-dress on his profile, with Hercules crowning him on the reverse. For the newly acquired territories in India proper Demetrius struck tetradrachms on the lower, Indian standard, portraying the king in what can best be described as a solar topee. The obverse inscription read in Greek: 'Of King Demetrius Aniketus' (invincible), while the reverse, showing Zeus, was inscribed in Kharoshthi script 'Of Maharajah Demetrius the Unconquered'

65

Syria Antiochus VI Dionysus 145–2 BC tetradrachm obv: radiate profile of king rev: the Dioscuri on prancing horses

— an interesting example of the blend of Greek and Indian cultures. Rectangular bronze coins bearing his profile were also struck, this format being popular in India.

Demetrius was ousted from Bactria by one of his generals, Eucratides, and from 175 to about 160 BC a series of wars was fought between Bactria and India, as Demetrius tried to regain his kingdom. From the Indian word Maharaja Eucratides adopted the epithet of 'great' which he added to the Greek word for king – the first European potentate to use this adjective. Eucratides is also noted for having minted the largest gold coin in classical times – a 20 stater piece weighing 169 grams. The only known example of this huge piece is now in the numismatic cabinet of the Bibliothèque Nationale in Paris. Towards the end of the second century BC Bactria was overrun by Indian tribes, though several petty states under Greek rulers survived in what are now Afghanistan and the Punjab for several years after.

Another portion of the Seleucid dominions which seceded to become an independent kingdom was Parthia (roughly coterminous with present-day Iran). Under Tiridates I drachmae portraying the king in a Persian head-dress and showing a seated Apollo on the reverse were struck. Similar types of profile and Apollo appeared in the reigns of his successors. About 160 BC Mithridates I greatly extended his kingdom and his successor Mithridates II annexed Mesopotamia in about 124 BC. During this period the tetradrachms and drachmae featured Greek gods and demigods – Zeus, Tyche or Hercules – but latterly the Greek element in the

a tetradrachm of Gotarzes (40–51 AD); *b* tetradrachm of Phraates IV (37–2 BC); *c* drachma of Mithridates II (123–88 BC) old head; *d* drachma of Sinatruces (77–70 BC); *e* drachma of Mithridates II (123–88 BC) young head. All reverses show Arsaces, founder of the dynasty, seated and holding a bow coins of Parthia decreased significantly. By the time of Orodes II in the middle of the first century BC the coins of Parthia had lost their Grecian simplicity and were cluttered with verbose inscriptions of which 'King of kings, Arsaces the Benefactor, the Just, God Manifest, Philhellene [Greek-lover]' is a typical example. Although the Hellenistic kingdom of Parthia was not overthrown by the Persians till 22 AD its coins had long since ceased to be Greek in any respect.

Several kingdoms were established in Asia Minor in the early years of the third century BC, in Pontus, Pergamum and Bithynia, all of which struck Attic tetradrachms which exhibited varying degrees of eclecticism. In many respects the Hercules-Zeus pattern of Alexandrian coinage was followed, though Mithridates III of Pontus replaced Hercules with his own portrait, and added his personal emblem, the crescent and star to the Zeus reverse. It is interesting to note that the badge of Mithridates was subsequently adopted by the Byzantine empire from which it passed to the Turks and is still used throughout the Moslem world. Various Greek deities appeared on the coins of his successors but Mithridates VI produced staters and tetradrachms with allegorical types and animal emblems such as a stag or Pegasus. A rather stylised profile of Alexander the Great was used on staters minted for Pontus in Byzantium and the Black Sea ports. The coinage of Bithynia followed a stereotyped pattern of royal profiles, with reverse types featuring a seated goddess or a standing figure of Zeus. Both Pontus and Bithynia came to an end in 74 BC when they were annexed to the Roman Empire.

The kingdom of Pergamum arose out of the Aegean coast of Asia Minor, having broken away from the Seleucid empire about 287 BC, though continuing to acknowledge the suzerainty of Seleucus I whose features appeared on the earliest coins of Pergamum, with a seated figure of Athena on the reverse. These coins, however, bore the name of Philetaerus, whose nephew Eumenes I, on succeeding him in 263 BC, broke away from the Seleucids and transferred his allegiance to Egypt. On the coins of Eumenes the portrait of Philetaerus was substituted, though Athena was retained for the reverse. During the reign of Attalus I, another nephew of Philetaerus, the famous cistophoric (chest-bearing) coinage of Pergamum was initiated. These tetradrachms derived their name from the chest which was depicted on the obverse, with a serpent crawling from under its half-open lid. The reverse showed a bow-case flanked by serpents and variety was imparted by the inclusion of civic emblems, mintmarks and magistrates' initials. Despite their ugliness the *cistophoroi* eventually became very popular all over Asia Minor and were struck at a large number of mints in Ionia, Phrygia, Lydia and Mysia as well as Pergamum itself. Such was the popularity of these coins that they continued to be minted long after Asia Minor had become a Roman province and, indeed, they survived to the end of the pre-Christian era.

The last, but by no means the least, of the post-Alexandrian kingdoms was Egypt. The rulers of Egypt could claim direct descent from the kings of Macedon, which was more than the other successors to Alexander could say. The founder of the Egyptian kingdom was Ptolemy Soter who initially governed as satrap in the names of Philip III and Alexander IV. Like Lysimachus in Thrace, Ptolemy was content to substitute for Hercules a deified portrait of Alexander the Great wearing an elephant head-dress and decorated with a Grecian aegis. The Zeus reverse type was superseded about 315 BC by a warlike figure of Athena. Alexander's name was still inscribed on the reverse, but now Ptolemy's emblem, an eagle, was also added. Some of these coins even bore a Greek inscription signifying 'an Alexandrian coin of Ptolemy'. After the death of Alexander IV in 310 Ptolemy dropped the pretence of allegiance to the Alexandrian ideal. Within five years he had assumed the title of king and placed his own profile on the coins of Egypt. The Ptolemaic coins varied considerably in weight as Egypt first abandoned the Attic standard for the Chian and then dabbled with the Cyrene standard, that city becoming one of the chief Egyptian mints, the others being at Alexandria and Salamis in Cyprus. The gold staters and silver tetradrachms of the latter part of Ptolemy's reign bore his portrait on the obverse and a chariot drawn by four elephants on the reverse.

His son and successor, Ptolemy II (usually known as Philadelphus – 'sister-lover' – on account of his incestuous marriage to

a Egypt gold pentadrachm 285–246 BC obv: Ptolemy I; *b* Egypt gold tetradrachm 285–246 BC obv: Ptolemy II and Arsinoe

a   b

his sister, Arsinoe) continued the coin types of his father, but in 271 BC began striking staters bearing the conjoined profiles of his parents on the obverse and profiles of himself and his sister on the other. Following Arsinoe's death in 270 BC coins appeared with her portrait in deified form. A double cornucopia, with the Greek inscription 'of brother-loving Arsinoe' appeared on the reverse. For a short time Cyrenaica seceded from Egypt, but they were brought together again in 258 BC when Ptolemy III married Berenice, daughter of Maga, a half-brother of Ptolemy II who had seceded from Egypt. Ptolemy III ruled jointly with his father till 246 BC when Philadelphus died. Gold eight-drachmae pieces were minted at Ephesus and bore the profile of Berenice and a cornucopia, on obverse and reverse respectively. During the latter part of the reign of Ptolemy III, down to 221 BC, gold coins in units of ten, five, two-and-a-half and a quarter drachmae, and silver in denominations of ten, five and two-and-a-half drachmae were struck with a profile of Berenice.

Ptolemy IV Philopator (father-loving) succeeded his father in 221 BC and shortly afterwards removed his mother's influence by having her murdered. During his reign Ptolemy IV practised the cult of the ancient Egyptian gods Serapis and Isis and placed their effigies on his silver tetradrachms, while reserving for himself and his wife the places of honour on the gold octodrachms. He was followed on the throne by his infant son, Ptolemy V, in 204 BC. During the minority of this king Egypt's more powerful neighbour, Syria, took the opportunity to wrest from Egypt all her foreign territory, except Cyprus and Cyrenaica. Even after

70

a Egypt tetradrachm of Askalon 49 BC obv: Cleopatra VII (69–30 BC) rev: eagle; *b* Egypt tetradrachm 32 BC obv: Cleopatra VII rev: Antony

a

b

Ptolemy V married Cleopatra, daughter of the Seleucid king Antiochus the Great, Egypt's troubles did not cease. In 181 BC Ptolemy V died and Cleopatra became regent for her young son Ptolemy VI. Cleopatra's brother, Antiochus VI, invaded Egypt itself. None of these disastrous events found reflection on the coins of Egypt which, during these and the succeeding reigns, continued to use the familiar portrait types. During this period large bronze coins, bearing the same devices, were struck at Alexandria. One result of the Seleucid invasion, however, was the introduction of this type of bronze coinage into Syria under Antiochus VI.

During the latter half of the second century BC Egypt was not only beset by trouble from beyond its frontiers but troubled by political chaos within. In 146 BC Ptolemy VII was murdered by his uncle who took the title of Ptolemy VIII. Numismatically, Ptolemy VIII's reign is noteworthy for the dates, in regnal years, which appeared on his coins. Following his death in 116 BC a regency was established under Cleopatra III who proved too weak and incompetent to prevent numerous contenders for the throne engaging in civil war in pursuance of their claims. Peace was not restored till 80 BC when Ptolemy XIII ascended the throne. Despite his grandiloquent pose as heir to the ancient pharaohs this king cut a comic figure, particularly among his Greek subjects who dismissed him contemptuously as 'the Flute-player'. His coins were likewise contemptible, both in intrinsic content and in subject-matter, with their crude effigies of Ptolemy I.

The last of the Ptolemies was the daughter of the Flute-player, Cleopatra VII, who reigned from 51 to 30 BC. Not only did she give back to Egypt for a brief period something of its pristine glory but also, for a time, wielded considerable influence over the eastern dominions of the Roman Republic, as a result of the magnetic effect she had on Mark Antony. Although posterity has long regarded her as one of the great beauties of all time the portraits on her coins belie this. The silver tetradrachms struck on her behalf in Antioch depict her as a beaky individual with a haughty countenance. Admittedly the quality of the engraving is inferior and, by contrast, the handsome drachmae of Alexandria are more flattering. These coins, and some large pieces of about the same period, portray her as a young woman in her early twenties and manage to convey something of her irresistible charm rather than create an effect of matchless beauty. The last coins to portray Cleopatra belong more properly to the second half of this book since they were minted under the authority of Antony and bear his portrait on one side and hers on the other. On these denarii, struck about 34 BC, she is shown in a singularly unflattering pose. Cleopatra and her Roman lover did not long survive their disastrous confrontation with Octavian at the sea-battle of Actium in 31 BC and within months she ended her life by her own hand. There was a certain glamour about the way in which the last of the Alexandrian kingdoms came to an end. Henceforward the coinage of this area, like the rest of the classical world, was mainly Roman.

6 the last vestiges of greek coinage

Mention has been made in the preceding chapter of the successors to the empire of Alexander the Great and how, eventually, their kingdoms were absorbed into the Roman sphere of influence, usually bringing their distinctive coinage to an end. The same pattern of events overtook the Greek cities of Sicily and Magna Graecia although, on account of their proximity to Rome, their assimilation into the Roman dominions occurred much earlier and therefore their coins came to an end much sooner.

At the beginning of the fourth century Sicily and Magna Graecia were still independent of Rome and, indeed, the principal enemy at that time was Carthage which had attempted several invasions of Sicily and southern Italy. In 310 BC Agathocles, the autocratic ruler of New Syracuse, even invaded North Africa and struck a powerful blow at the Carthaginian homeland. To celebrate his three-year campaign in North Africa Agathocles struck silver tetradrachms with the virgin-goddess Kore on the obverse and a figure of Victory on the reverse. While campaigning in Africa he issued gold staters modelled on those of Ptolemy I Soter, with whom he was allied against the Carthaginians. In 304 BC he emulated the Alexandrian generals and assumed the title of *Basileus* (king) which henceforward was inscribed on his coins. Conversely this war left its effect on the coins of Carthage which minted tetradrachms with a profile of Hercules on the obverse and the usual Punic reverse of a horse and palm tree.

In the early years of the third century the Carthaginians

a Zeugitania, Carthage electrum stater *c.* 241–146 BC obv: Persephone;
b Syracuse 8 litra 216–215 BC obv: head of Gelon II

a   b

launched a fresh attack on Sicily and Hicetas, ruler of Syracuse, appealed to Pyrrhus, king of Epirus, for assistance. Pyrrhus had earlier come to the aid of the people of Magna Graecia in their war with Rome in 282 BC. It was in that campaign, incidentally, that Pyrrhus defeated the Romans but suffered tremendous losses, thus giving rise to the expression 'a Pyrrhic victory' for a dearly won battle. Pyrrhus was more successful four years later when he was proclaimed king of Sicily in order to prosecute the war against Carthage more effectively. Coins bearing his name were struck at Syracuse. This campaign proved to be indecisive and after three years Pyrrhus abandoned Sicily to its fate, returning eventually to his own kingdom in Epirus. One of his ablest generals was elected to rule Sicily in his place. Under the wise guidance of Hieron II Sicily enjoyed a comparatively long period of stability. The coins of his reign consisted initially of *pegasi* bearing his name and latterly of coins depicting his profile. Several members of his family were also portrayed on Syracusan coins – a precedent later followed by the Roman emperors. He was succeeded in 216 BC by his grandson, Hieronymus, who proved to be a most unpopular ruler and was assassinated within a year. Syracuse reverted to republican government and formed an alliance with Hannibal against Rome in the Second Punic War. Sicily suffered as a result of Hannibal's defeat, Syracuse being captured by the Romans in 212 BC. With the incorporation of Sicily into the Roman state in that year distinctive coinage came to an end.

74

a Aspendus stater third century BC obv: two wrestlers rev: slinger in action; *b* Troas, Abydus *c*. 196 BC tetradrachm obv: Artemis rev: eagle and bee

Both the Alexandrian and the Roman empires permitted certain Greek cities and local confederations to continue minting their own coinage for local use. Thus under the Alexandrian generals and their successors there were several 'free' cities which managed to preserve some semblance of autonomy by playing off one ruler against another. The most important of these cities were Athens and Sparta on the mainland of Greece, while the Aegean island of Rhodes wielded considerable power not only over its neighbours but also over a large portion of the hinterland of Asia Minor. It is curious that Sparta, which never had any use for coinage in the accepted sense during the heyday of the Greek city-states, should begin to strike coins in the third century. These coins were Attic-weight tetradrachms of the Alexandrian type but bearing the name of Areus, king of Sparta. While Areus was content to feature Alexander the Great and the seated Zeus on his coins, his illustrious successor, Cleomenes, chose a profile of himself, modelled closely on the coins of Antiochus II and bearing a Seleucid Apollo on the reverse. Later coins of Sparta continued to be strongly influenced by the Seleucid empire. The coins of an

75

autonomous Sparta bore the profile of King Nabis with Hercules on the reverse. The Spartans were defeated and absorbed into the Achaean League in 192 BC and subsequently used the coins of that confederacy, dealt with more fully later in this chapter.

By contrast Athens maintained her independence only at sporadic intervals from the fourth century onwards, being often the subject of attack by conflicting forces in the Hellenistic kingdoms which succeeded the empire of Alexander. Yet, with the possible exception of the period between 262 and 255 BC (when Athens was under Macedonian military occupation), this city continued to mint its famous tetradrachms featuring Athena and her owl. Though no longer a powerful sovereign state Athens was, in the third century BC, the most prosperous commercial centre in Greece and the focal point of Greek learning and culture. It was on these grounds that the kings and generals who conquered and occupied the city in turn allowed the civic authorities the privilege of minting their own coins. The late tetradrachms were smaller and lighter than the fourth-century pieces and generally more finely executed, though lacking the robust artistry of the earlier coins. Furthermore these later 'owls' have a cluttered appearance, as magistrates' names, initials and symbols were added haphazardly to the reverse. Athenian coins were even imitated in the second century BC by the cities of Crete who were allied with Athens and Rome against Macedon; these 'owls' may be distinguished from the Athenian coins by the tiny civic emblems of the Cretan towns. In the middle of the second century 'owls' were imitated by the Ionian cities and scholars have even traced the likeness of the Athenian coinage in the silver pieces struck by the Himyarites of south Arabia at the end of the second century.

In 88 BC Athens sided with King Mithridates of Pontus against Rome and suffered defeat at the hands of Sulla. Although Athens now became a Roman dependency Sulla continued to mint Athenian tetradrachms, placing on the reverse two trophies flanking the owl, to commemorate his victories over Mithridates at Chaeronea and Orchomenos in 86 and 85 BC. Incredibly Athens continued to strike her familiar 'owls' for another sixty years, although her commercial importance was sadly impaired by the destruction of the port of Piraeus in 86 BC. Nevertheless her

Rhodes tetradrachm *c.* 304–166 BC obv: Helios rev: rose-bud

position as custodian of Greek culture, which the Romans admired, gave Athens a privileged status symbolised by the continuance of her coins long after all the other cities and states of the Greek world had been forced to close down their mints. Even Augustus, the first Roman emperor, who reorganised the coinage used throughout his vast dominions, did not dare to suppress the coins of Athens. In the end, however, the silver lodes of Laurium were exhausted and the last diminutive drachmae were struck in 25 BC – a rather pathetic and ignominious conclusion to almost 600 years of continuous numismatic activity.

Her geographic situation enabled the island of Rhodes to maintain her independence throughout the third and the first half of the second centuries. Just as the Knights of St John more than a thousand years later were able to withstand the might of the Ottomans by means of their powerful navy, so the Rhodians of the post-Alexandrian era became a formidable force in the eastern Mediterranean and the Aegean by means of their deadly battle-fleet. Rhodes was an important ally of Rome in her struggle against the Seleucid empire. During the period from 305 to 167 BC Rhodes minted gold staters, halves and quarters and silver didrachms and tetradrachms featuring the full-face portrait of Helios the sun-god on the obverse and the rose (*rhodos*) on the reverse. The portrait of Helios was an allusion to the 100-foot high Colossus of Rhodes which bestrode the entrance to the harbour and was regarded as one of the Seven Wonders of the World. Although Rome subdued her former ally in 167 and deprived the island of its maritime power, Rhodes continued to produce its own coins at infrequent intervals, though the majority

77

of these were merely bronze tokens with no more than local validity.

In the tangled politics of Greece in the aftermath of Alexander's empire there arose two leagues or confederacies which enjoyed ephemeral autonomy and struck their own coins. The Aetolian League came to prominence in 279 BC when the cities of Aetolia repelled a Gaulish invasion of Greece. To celebrate this victory the Aetolians minted gold staters and half-staters portraying Athena and Hercules on the respective obverses, with a representation of the Aetolian victory memorial at Delphi on both reverses. The Aetolian League also minted silver tetradrachms portraying Hercules on the obverse and showing a seated figure on the reverse, not unlike the Zeus of the Alexandrian coins.

At about the same time a similar league was established in the Peloponnese. The Achaean League, modelled on the earlier league of the same name which had flourished briefly in the early fourth century under the leadership of Epaminondas of Thebes, was re-formed about 280 BC when the cities of Dyme and Patrae rose against their Macedonian overlords and drove out their garrisons. Within thirty years the majority of Peloponnesian cities had joined this league, which continued to strike coins down to 146 BC when it was overthrown by the Romans. The uniform coinage of this league consisted of silver triobols (half drachmae) featuring a profile of Zeus on the obverse and the wreathed monogram AX (initials of Achaea) on the reverse, with the symbol of the issuing city. Large bronze coins were also produced, with a standing Zeus on the obverse and a seated female figure (symbolising Achaea) on the reverse.

Under the Roman empire many Greek cities were allowed to strike bronze coins for local circulation. The fabric and appearance of these coins had a certain uniformity: invariably a profile of the emperor on the obverse and an allegorical subject of local importance on the reverse. Notable exceptions were Macedonia and Athens which were permitted on certain occasions to use portraits of Alexander and Athena respectively. Inscriptions on these bronze coins continued to be rendered in Greek, and particularly interesting are the often grandiloquent epithets by which the issuing cities liked to describe themselves – 'illustrious'

Damascus, 'brilliant' Syedra, or 'greatest and best' Nicaea, while other places bore epithets alluding to their naval or religious importance. These bronze coins survived as late as 268 AD, by which time the depreciation of Roman Imperial coinage had gone so far that the continuance of local bronze coins became utterly pointless.

7 the roman republic 269-30 BC

Until fairly recently most reference works on the subject of Roman coins stated quite categorically that Rome did not begin to use coins until 269 BC. A few went further and stated that in that year the first of the long series of silver denarii made their appearance – thereby repeating a curious error perpetrated as long ago as the historian Pliny the Elder in the first century BC. It is true that coins as we know them coincided with the establishment of the Roman Mint in 269 BC but it would have been surprising if the Romans had not produced money of some sort at an earlier date. What is more surprising, however, is that, bearing in mind the beautiful and prolific silver coinage of the cities and seaports of Magna Graecia, the Romans were not influenced by this more strongly at an earlier date.

It must be remembered that, prior to the Punic Wars, Rome had not yet emerged as a powerful force beyond the limits of northern and central Italy and, at the beginning of the third century, Rome and her allies were at a far lower level of sophistication and commercial development than the Greek colonies of Sicily and the south. Even so, the Romans had, by this time, progressed beyond the reckoning of wealth according to cattle though the word for money (*pecunia*) was derived from the word for a herd (*pecus*). Silver was comparatively scarce in the early Roman world and it was more natural that the first metallic substitute for wealth should be bronze. Initially this was computed solely by weight and the bronze was carted around in huge, uneven lumps, irregular in size and weight, so that it would have been necessary to weigh them out at each transaction. Our word *spend* – applied to money – originated in this curious way, from the Latin *expendere* – to weigh out (derived in turn from *ex*, meaning out, and *pondus*, meaning weight). From *pondus* we also get the word *pound* which, in English, can be either a weight (lb) or a monetary value (£). The Romans themselves were more specific and used the word *libra* to denote a pound weight, though from this comes the modern Italian unit of currency, the *lira*, indicated in prices by exactly the same symbol adopted for the pound sterling.

The large irregular lumps of bronze were known succinctly as *Aes rude* (rough bronze). Gradually these pieces became more uniform in appearance, taking the shape of rectangular ingots. By the beginning of the third century BC it was becoming customary to make these ingots of an even weight, approximately five pounds. To guarantee both the quality and weight of these bars, so that it would no longer be necessary to weigh them laboriously at each transaction, they were impressed on both sides with the stamp of authority. These pieces were known as *Aes signatum* (signed bronze) and it has been conjectured that they probably made their first appearance in or about 289 BC when a commission of three was appointed 'for the purpose of casting and striking bronze, silver and gold'. Among the various devices stamped on these bars was that showing a bull – perhaps a direct reference to the origins of Roman currency. An extremely interesting type of *Aes signatum* is that with an elephant struck on the obverse and a pig on the reverse – an allusion to the battle of Beneventum in 274 BC when the elephants employed by Pyrrhus were panicked by the smell of the pigs driven by the Romans against them.

The *Aes signatum* gave way to *Aes grave* (heavy bronze) which were cast in circular form and weighed anything up to a pound. The largest piece of *Aes grave* was called an *As* and smaller denominations consisted of subdivisions according to weight. An interesting feature of the heavy bronze pieces was the inclusion of a symbol indicating the denomination. A Roman numeral I appeared on the *As* itself, the basic unit of currency. Half of this was the *Semis*, indicated by the letter S. The smallest subdivision

Denarius 268–180 BC obv: helmeted profile of Roma rev: Castor and Pollux

of the As was the twelfth or *Uncia* (our word ounce) and its value was indicated by a small pellet like a full stop. The values between the *Semis* and the *Uncia* were the third (*Triens*), quarter (*Quadrans*) and sixth (*Sextans*) indicated by four, three and two pellets respectively. The *Aes grave* series which made its debut at Rome in 269 BC was transitional in a sense that it ran parallel to the heavy bronze currencies of the other Latin districts and bridged the gap between the lumps and ingots of an earlier generation and the coins of the middle of the third century. But contemporaneous with the heavy bronze series there appeared silver coins for the first time. These consisted of four different types of didrachms, usually with smaller denominations of litra, half-litra and the silver as. Ten asses of silver or bronze were the equivalent of one didrachm.

The first of the didrachms bore the inscription ROMANO (thought to be a decayed form of *Romanorum* – 'of the Romans'). In design the influence of the Greek cities of southern Italy was strong: it has even been suggested that Greek craftsmen were responsible for engraving the dies and striking the coins. Deities and heroes of mythology – Hercules, Mars, Minerva, Apollo, Diana and the two-headed Janus – were the more popular subjects. The coins of the ROMANO class have been arranged by numismatists into four series according to type and weight relationship but, with the exception of series A which has been attributed to the mint at Rome itself, attempts at assigning these series to specific mints have only been conjectural. It is likely that the other ROMANO sets were struck by allies of Rome.

Round about 235 BC the ROMANO coins gave way to a new, and somewhat smaller series bearing the inscription ROMA. As before, these didrachms had their subdivisions of litra, half litra and as, together with a heavy bronze series for smaller denominations. The ROMA series was produced after the Roman victory in the First Punic War, and the straitened financial circumstances of Rome in the aftermath of war help to explain the fact that the weights of the coins, both silver and bronze, had to be reduced. As with the ROMANO coins, there were four series of the ROMA didrachms and lesser denominations, but again, nothing is known for certain regarding the mints which issued them. We can be fairly certain, however, that the series A, portraying Janus on the obverses, emanated from Rome itself. When the first war with Carthage came to an end, shortly before these coins appeared, the doors on the temple of Janus were closed to signify that Rome was at peace; and it was no doubt to celebrate this that the profile of Janus was chosen for the didrachm and silver as of Rome. The silver coins of what we might term the subsidiary mints died out within a decade and, about the same time, the weight system of heavy bronze was reduced by half, the bronze as being now about 136 grams, or half a Roman *libra* in weight. During the Second Punic War the weight of the heavy bronze coins was reduced yet again, to a third of what it had been originally.

Rome's first gold coinage appeared in 216 BC. Paradoxically this was an emergency issue, produced in wartime when stocks of silver for more conventional coins were running low. These coins consisted of staters and half-staters, respectively depicting Janus and two warriors swearing an oath of alliance over a pig held by a third warrior. Even after the war provisional issues of gold coins were made, in 211 BC and 209 BC, to alleviate the shortage of silver. The coins of the postwar period passed current as 20, 40 or 60 asses. They depicted Mars, god of war, on the obverse, with his attributes, the eagle and thunderbolt, on the reverse, and bore Roman numerals to signify their value. During the war a small silver coin of drachma value but usually known as a *victoriate*, from the figure of Victory on the obverse, was struck. Inflation caused by the war led to a fall in the value of the didrachm, until it vanished altogether and was replaced by the victoriate. The early victoriates, presumably all minted at Rome, had no distinctive mint marks, but later the sub-types of this coin proliferated and may be found with code letters and symbols indicating their production at mints in other parts of Italy or the Roman sphere of influence, as far afield as Corcyra (Corfu) and Sardinia.

The defeat of Carthage in the Second Punic War saw the emergence of Rome as the greatest power in the Mediterranean, but one impoverished by the strain on her resources, which called for a reorganisation of the economic structure. This was reflected in the monetary reforms which took place about 211 BC and saw the introduction of a new coinage based on the silver denarius. The denarius – ancestor of the medieval denier and the dinar used, to the present day, from Yugoslavia to the Persian Gulf, and preserved in British currency by the abbreviation *d* used for a penny – was a small silver coin weighing 4·5 grams and divided into ten asses, the bronze as being now a mere sixth of a pound in weight. The denarius was divided into the quinarius (five asses) and the sestertius (two and a half asses). Curiously enough in 'money of account' it was the sestertius, rather than the denarius, which was used. Large sums of money were reckoned in sestertii; if someone said that he was worth 80,000, sestertii would be understood, not denarii.

The basic types of the denarius remained fairly constant over a long period, with the helmeted profile of Roma or Bellona on the obverse and the Heavenly Twins (*Dioscuri*) Castor and Pollux on the reverse. The Dioscuri had a special significance for the Romans since it was traditionally believed that their timely intervention on the Roman side had saved the day at the Battle of Lake Regillus in 497 BC. The same designs bore, in addition, the symbols Q (quinarius) and IIs (*duo et semis*: two and a half). The Roman numeral X (ten) appeared on the denarius itself to indicate its value in asses. The corresponding bronze series ranged from the as to the semuncia (half ounce), and had a standard reverse showing the prow of a ship, and various gods and goddesses portrayed on the obverses. The weight of the bronze coins was progressively reduced during the second century BC and by about

Bronze as 150 BC obv: double-head of Janus rev: galley prow

155 BC the as had shrunk to an ounce. In the silver series the humble sestertius soon vanished from circulation, though it remained in popular parlance, in much the same way as the English guinea was retained in commercial usage for more than 150 years after it ceased to exist as an actual coin.

During the second century BC the power struggle between Rome and Carthage moved inexorably to its climax, the Third Punic War and the destruction of Carthage in 146 BC. The protracted struggle for supremacy in the Mediterranean inevitably had repercussions on the economy of Rome and resulted yet again in gradual reductions in the coinage. About 155 BC the denarius reached its minimum weight of four grams and subtle changes were made in the design of the reverse. The Heavenly Twins, who had graced the reverse of the denarius since its inception, were now gradually supplanted on the denarius and its subsidiary coins by the goddess Diana and subsequently other gods and goddesses appeared.

Hitherto an elaborate system of letters and symbols had been used to indicate the date or sequence of the issue of the coins, but these were now replaced by the initials of the magistrates under whose authority the coins were minted. At first only an initial or monogram was used but gradually part of a name would appear and in the end the inscriptions of the moneyers were quite lengthy and tended to clutter up the design. From the numismatic, rather than the aesthetic, viewpoint, however, the inscriptions on the reduced denarii of 155 BC onwards are a useful and invariably accurate means of dating the coins. After the destruction of Carthage, Diana the Huntress was superseded on the reverse by an allegorical figure representing Victory driving a two-horse chariot. These Victory denarii and similar types featuring Jupiter, Mars, Juno, Hercules and other mythological figures were in use down to 124 BC. The stock reverses showing major deities gradually gave way to more varied treatment. Just as the moneyers assumed greater importance, in that their names appeared on the coins, so also they were in a position to decide on the designs especially the reverse types. The subjects they chose often alluded to myths and legends connected with their families. The wolf with Romulus and Remus, for example, was chosen for the coins struck under the authority of Sextus Pompilius Fostlus, an allusion to the tradition that it was his ancestor, the shepherd Faustulus, who discovered the she-wolf with the twins.

In the generation following the defeat of Carthage the Romans began their meteoric expansion beyond the Italian peninsula, into Gaul and Iberia, North Africa and across the Adriatic into Greece. At home politics were marked by the rise and fall of the brothers Gaius and Tiberius Gracchus. Among the many reforms which they instituted during their tenure of various high offices in the administration of the Republic was the retariffing of the denarius, in 124 BC, at sixteen instead of ten asses. A legacy of this division, carried out at a time when the bronze as was nominally worth an ounce, is the system of weights used in Britain and the English-speaking world to this day, of the pound avoirdupois divided into sixteen ounces. At the time of the Gracchi's currency reforms, however, the bronze as in fact ceased to be minted and existed only as money of account, though the lesser bronze denominations, from semis to uncia, continued to appear. The change in value of the denarius was indicated by the incorporation of the numerals XVI, transformed after a time into an asterisk symbol. A curious feature of the fabric of denarii in the closing years of the second century BC was the notching of the rim, a device which was intended to demonstrate that the coin was silver to its core and not 'clad' or plated. Accusations of debasing the currency were frequently levelled at the government by the opposition parties and the serration of the coin edges was supposed to be an effective

86

proof of good faith. Nevertheless excellent base metal forgeries have been discovered in which a thin silver wash has effectively overcome the problem of the notched edge.

During the second century BC, as the power of Rome increased and the land around the Mediterranean was brought under her control, it became necessary to produce coins for the colonies in the territory itself and subsidiary mints were established in Gaul and Spain. In general the coins struck outside Rome followed the designs of the metropolis and from the evidence of coin hoards found in these areas it would seem likely that coinage was only produced when necessity demanded, as, for example, during the Cimbrian War (101 BC) and the campaign against Jugurtha (110 BC). In fabric the 'colonial' issues were invariably thinner and wider than those of Rome and the effigies consequently in comparatively low relief.

The designs of the coins produced by the Roman Republic in the latter half of the second century BC became increasingly varied and the somewhat stereotyped traditions of Diana and the Heavenly Twins gave way to more interesting subjects, often, as has already been noted, alluding to the history and traditions of the moneyer's family. The allusions are often obscure and an intimate knowledge of Roman history and mythology is required to unravel them. Continuing in the mythological vein of earlier issues is the denarius of the moneyer Sextus Julius Caesar showing Venus and Cupid – a reference to the tradition that the Julian family was descended from Aeneas, son of the goddess of love. More and more moneyers, however, took definite historical subjects for their reverse types and, for the first time, persons who had actually lived were featured. With the notable exception of some Macedonian gold staters of 197 BC, which portrayed the Roman general Flaminius in honour of his successful campaign against Mithridates, no living person was to appear on coins of the Roman world till the civil wars of the first century. But the way for the coins of Pompey and Julius Caesar was paved by the moneyers of the previous generation concentrating increasingly on personalities and less and less on allegorical symbolism.

At the beginning of the first century BC friction between Rome and her Italian allies flared up into the Social War of 91–88 BC,

so-called since the former allies (*socii*) – Apulia, Picenum and
Samnium – were ranged against Rome. The allies minted their
own denarii, inscribed in Latin or Oscan characters, and though
the majority of these coins were vaguely modelled on Roman
originals it is interesting to note that some pieces bore the
inscription ITALIA, thereby anticipating the coins of modern Italy
by two thousand years. The symbolism on these coins was
particularly apt – a bull (Italy) treading on a she-wolf (Rome).
During the period of the Social War prolific issues were made in
Rome itself, presenting a bewildering array of sub-types and long
series distinguished mainly by their sequence symbols. In particular the coins of the moneyers L. Piso Frugi and D. Junius Silanus
exhibit numerous minor differences which have been tabulated in
chronological sequence by numismatic scholars. Apart from the
vast issues of denarii at this time the main innovations were the
re-introduction of the silver sestertius and the bronze as, the latter
now shrunk to half an ounce in weight.

The revolt of the former allies fizzled out in 88 BC but in its
place Rome was suddenly faced with troubles from within. The
internal dissensions between the senatorial and democratic parties,
temporarily dormant during the Social War flared up as soon as
the Italian Confederation collapsed. Matters came to a head when
Sulla marched on Rome, occupied the city and defeated the
democratic party. Once the senatorial faction was safely in power
Sulla departed to take up command of the expedition against
Mithridates of Pontus. No sooner had he left Rome than his chief

opponent Marius staged a counter-revolution resulting in the defeat of the senatorial party and the return of the democrats. The political upheavals of the years 88–82 BC were reflected to some extent in the coins of the period, insofar as the four moneyers who issued coins under Sulla were rapidly superseded by another three under Marius. These men, in turn, were replaced by another group of three who took the unusual step of placing their names on the same coins, though the order in which they were inscribed varies. Coins bearing the names of all three moneyers were also produced after the return of Sulla and the defeat of the Marian faction in 82 BC. For three years Sulla ruled dictatorially and during this period the issues of the moneyers, both jointly and individually, contain an enormous variety of sequence marks. It remains to be noted that Sulla struck his owns coins during his campaigns in Greece and Anatolia, the work being carried out at local Greek mints. The most notable of these coins were the gold *aurei*, thought to have been minted at Athens, which show Roma on the obverse and Sulla in a four-horse chariot on the reverse. The winged figure of Victory incorporated in this reverse is an allusion to Sulla's defeat of Mithridates. Silver denarii were also produced in Gaul and Spain during this period, under the authority of the field commanders who led various expeditions against rebel units supporting the Marian faction. During the campaign against Sertorius the pro-Marius governor of Spain, C. Caecilius Metellus Pius, struck coins having an obverse type of Piety (a reference to his title Pius) and a reverse showing an elephant, emblem of the Caecilian family.

Sulla abdicated in 79 BC and died a year later. His demise was the signal for the democratic party to stage another comeback and the senatorial faction turned for help to one of Sulla's chief lieutenants, Sextus Pompeius Magnus, usually known as Pompey the Great. Pompey first achieved fame as an able general in the campaign against Mithridates, and it was he who eventually defeated Sentorius in Spain. During the years of the democratic ascendancy which followed the death of Sulla, Pompey was campaigning abroad, combating the pirates of the Mediterranean and generally biding his time. In 61 BC he returned to Rome, where he was accorded a 'triumph', the equivalent of the ticker-tape welcome in America today, and with the return of the senatorial party to power Pompey's influence on affairs of state increased rapidly. Pompey's return to Rome was marked by the issue of a gold coin featuring the allegorical representation of Africa (where his more recent campaigns had been conducted) with the inscription 'Magnus' (the Great) conferred on him in recognition of his military prowess. The reverse shows Pompey standing in a four-horse chariot. This very rare coin is significant numismatically since, for the first time, a living person was depicted on a coin struck at Rome itself.

Nevertheless the general practice of drawing on events and characters in the history of the moneyer's family continued, though significantly the incidents and persons depicted tended to be of more recent vintage, even within living memory. Thus Sulla appeared on coins struck a mere eighteen years after his death, when his son Faustus was moneyer. The coins of M. Scaurus show the surrender of the Nabataean king Aretas to Scaurus, an event which took place earlier in the latter's career, when he was Pompey's legate in the East in 62 BC. Of particular interest, in view of his subsequent career, are the gold and silver coins struck under the authority of Julius Caesar during his lengthy military campaigns in Gaul. Among these special mention must be made of a series of 50 BC which bear the Roman numerals LII, a reference to Caesar's age at the time of the issue. Few attempts had been made at dating coins according to their year of issue and the use of Caesar's age as a means of reckoning is all the more remarkable. This device was an indication of the growing 'cult of personality' which was soon to be taken to its logical conclusion – the appearance of a profile of a living ruler on the obverse of coins, instead of relegating the figure of a human being to a relatively minor role on the reverse.

The long dictatorship of Pompey came to an end in 49 BC when Julius Caesar, in answer to pleas from the opposition party in Rome, decided to return from campaigning abroad. Once he had crossed the Rubicon – an expression which has become proverbial for irrevocable decisions – there could be no turning back, though Caesar seems to have had his moments of doubt at the time. His armies swept on to Rome, gaining support as they went, and

Pompey prudently withdrew to Greece. There followed five years of intermittent civil war, inconclusive in many respects, and though by 45 BC Pompey was dead and his sons defeated, resistance to Caesar lingered on in the remoter parts of the Roman dominions, particularly in North Africa and western Asia.

During this period the central authority of the Senate, in monetary as in other affairs, was challenged on numerous occasions. On both sides in the civil wars of 49–45 BC extensive series of coinage were struck by the various generals and military governors. Silver denarii form the bulk of this series, though quite a number of gold coins, as well as a not inconsiderable quantity of bronze, were produced. The historical allusions to the moneyer's family were still present but more and more there was a tendency to depict events connected with the war itself. This was especially true of the period following Pompey's death in 46 BC when judicious use of distinctive coin types was made by those who wished to keep alive the spirit of Pompey and perpetuate the memory of his exploits. Under his heirs and successors, Cnaeus and Sextus Pompeius, coins were struck in Spain bearing Pompey's profile on the obverse and an allegorical tableau on the reverse, showing the female figure of Hispania welcoming Cnaeus Pompey as he disembarked.

The coinage struck at Rome after Caesar's assumption of supreme power in 49 BC moved gradually from rather idealistic types with allegories of victory, peace, harmony and liberty, to more realistic types referring directly to Caesar himself. In particular the inscriptions on these coins became more extensive and, while referring less to the moneyer, referred increasingly to Caesar, in a recital of his various public offices: Consul, Dictator, Pontifex Maximus (chief priest – a title used to this day on papal coins), Imperator (in the literal sense of 'commander', not as 'emperor' as it later developed), and, last of all, Parens Patriae – 'Father of the Country' – which appeared on the coins struck in March 44 BC shortly before his assassination. Two important points in Roman numismatics occurred in the last of Caesar's coins. The commission or 'college' of moneyers was for the first time increased from three to four (they signed coins in pairs) and the pride of place on the obverse was occupied by the profile of the living Caesar.

a aureus of Sextus Pompey obv: Pompey the Great rev: Cnaeus and Sextus Pompey; *b* aureus of Julius Caesar obv: Roma rev: Victory and trophies; *c* Julius Caesar denarius 44 BC obv: Caesar rev: symbols of dictatorship mint-mark L. BUCA

a

b

c

The murder of Caesar on the Ides of March acted catalytically on the whole structure of the Roman world. Fifteen years were to pass before any single figure emerged sufficiently powerful to weld the heterogeneous elements together into a cohesive empire. In the immediate aftermath of Caesar's death the conspirators, Brutus and Cassius, fled to Greece where they maintained uneasy independence until their defeat at Philippi two years later. In Rome some semblance of law and order was created by the Triumvirate,

a denarius of Brutus obv: Brutus rev: daggers symbolizing Caesar's assassination; *b* aureus of the Triumvirate obv: Antony rev: Lepidus

a

b

composed of Mark Antony (Caesar's aide and fellow consul), Octavian (Caesar's grand-nephew and heir) and a relative nonentity Lepidus (Caesar's master-of-horse). This ill-matched trio were not to work amicably for long. At first they resolved their differences by dividing the Roman world among them: Gaul and the western provinces were apportioned to Antony, Lepidus was fobbed off with Africa while Octavian retained Greece and the eastern provinces and wielded effectual authority over Rome and Italy.

In the years immediately after Caesar's death coins (mostly silver but with an increasing number of gold issues) were struck at Rome for the Triumvirate or Octavian acting individually, in Gaul for Mark Antony and subsequently for Octavian when the latter ousted his rival there, in Egypt and Asia Minor by Antony after the break with Octavian became final in 40 BC, and in Greece by Brutus and Cassius before they were routed at Philippi in 42 BC. There were numerous military issues of a more ephemeral nature, including comparatively rare bronze coins under Antony for use by his Mediterranean fleet.

The old traditions of deities, and allusions to family events, characteristic of Roman coins down to this period, were finally superseded by obverse and reverse types primarily concerned with events as they happened. The first coins of Mark Antony, for example, struck for the Triumvirate at Rome shortly after Caesar's death, bore a veiled profile of Antony, an allusion to his mourning. Another obverse type of the same year shows the temple dedicated to Caesar's Clemency – the beginning of the procedure leading to Caesar's elevation to the status of a god. During the short-lived Triumvirate the college of moneyers, consisting of four men, individually produced two separate sets of coins each, one in gold and the other in a combination of gold and silver denominations. The gold and silver series were characterised by symbolic designs on both obverse and reverse, whereas the gold series bore portraits of the Triumvirs on the obverse and allegorical compositions allusive to particular Triumvirs on the reverse. The coins struck for Octavian trace the expansion of his power and influence at this time. The early reverse types showing Aeneas (referring to the traditional ancestry of the Julian family) gave way to designs bearing such symbols as a plough (alluding to the land settlements conferred by Octavian on war veterans in 41 BC. The inscription DIVI IVLI F. (son of the Divine Julius) begins to creep in, signifying both the deification of Caesar and the recognition of Octavian as his heir. The profile of Caesar also appeared increasingly as a reverse type on Octavian's coins, though he preferred to reserve for himself the place of honour on the obverse. The inscriptions on the later coins of Octavian, in the decade from 40 BC to 31 BC became increasingly complex, recording the multifarious public offices which he held. The progression of these inscriptions and the variations in the titles used serve as an accurate basis for the dating of these coins and placing them in the correct chronological sequence. A curious feature of the military issues struck for Octavian in Gaul in the early part of this decade was the incorporation in some instances of the profiles of Antony or Lepidus, though the alliance of the Triumvirs had all but ceased to exist.

In 45–42 BC Antony minted coins in Gaul which also made copious reference to his fellow Triumvirs. After the reorganisation of the provinces following the defeat of Brutus and Cassius the eastern provinces were assigned to Antony and numerous issues of coins were made under his authority in these areas. Among these is a series of gold coins portraying Antony with Octavia, sister of his co-Triumvir, whom he married in 40 BC. Despite the deterioration in their relationship Antony's coins continued to bear the name of Octavian as late as 37 BC. Antony's celebrated love affair with Cleopatra, Queen of Egypt, was reflected in the series of denarii minted at Alexandria after 34 BC. The last three years of Antony's power in the Eastern Mediterranean were marked by prolific issues of silver denarii and gold aurei extolling the virtues and prowess of his military forces. A lengthy series of denarii, whose silver content was minimal, was devoted to the various legions which served under his command. These legionary coins bear the regimental numbers from I to XXX on the reverse with an eagle emblem and military standards.

Dissension between Octavian and Antony arose over the spoils of war after Philippi. Octavian turned against Lucius, brother of Antony, and provoked the conflict known as the Perusine War (41–40 BC). Lucius was defeated and his family fled into exile. This action was scarcely calculated to endear Octavian to Antony, though the two men temporarily patched up their differences by the Treaty of Brundisium (Brindisi) in 40 BC. Antony married Octavian's sister Octavia but divorced her eight years later to marry Cleopatra. Octavian regarded this both as an insult and as a challenge. The Senate decreed Antony to have forfeited his command, and Octavian began preparing for a showdown with his former ally.

The final confrontation between Octavian and Antony came in 31 BC when the former led an expedition to the East. A great naval battle was fought at Actium in which Octavian emerged as sole and undisputed master of the Roman world. Antony and Cleopatra escaped but committed suicide a few months later. Octavian returned to Rome in triumph and marked the end of the long-continued anarchy and civil war by symbolically closing the doors on the temple of Janus. At the end of the year he formally surrendered the dictatorial powers which he had wielded for twelve years and a regular government, firmly under his control, was established. Nominally the Roman world was still a republic; in fact it had become an empire based on the autocracy of one man.

8 the roman empire
30 BC–295 AD

Although the battle of Actium must be regarded as one of the great decisive victories of world history the political status of the Roman world did not change overnight. Octavian was *de facto* ruler of the largest administrative bloc the world had ever known, extending from the North Sea to the Sahara, from the Danube to the Persian Gulf, but as yet he was careful to preserve the *de jure* government of the Republic, vested in the Senate and People of Rome, and the process by which he transferred this into a hereditary empire was gradually achieved. It was not, in fact, until 27 BC that the effective means of governing the hetero-geneous units of the Roman dominions had been evolved to Octavian's satisfaction. When he was sure of his position he resigned his extraordinary dictatorial status and accepted from the Senate the powers which established him as virtual emperor. As yet the term *imperator* had nothing more than a military connota-tion. Octavian, however, changed his name to Augustus and adopted the title of Caesar from his great-uncle. This surname was used as an indication of imperial rank, and in the forms Czar and Kaiser survived into the twentieth century.

During the transitional period before the emergence of the Roman empire, Octavian seems to have leaned over backwards to avoid undue self-promotion. After the spate of portrait coins in the years of the Triumvirate the issues of Rome and the other mints were comparatively bereft of profiles of Octavian, although copious reference was made, by means of symbol and allegory, to the victory at Actium and the re-unification of the Roman world.

Under Augustus some attempts were made to centralise coin production at Rome and, at the same time, a partial reform of the coinage was undertaken. The emphasis shifted from silver augmented by minor bronze coins to a bi-metallic system involving the regular use of gold for the higher denominations. The principal coin was the *denarius aureus* (literally 'gold penny'), usually referred to as an aureus, and its subdivision, the *quinarius aureus* or half aureus. Silver denarii were struck on a ratio of 25 to the aureus, with corresponding silver quinarii. The sestertius was revived as a brass coin, with its half piece, the *dupondius*. The *as* was re-tariffed at the rate of four, instead of two-and-a-half as previously, to the sestertius and struck in copper, while the lowest denomination of all was the *quadrans* or quarter-as, also minted in copper.

In his desire to base his autocracy on republican institutions Augustus was content to derive his power from his vaguely defined position as *princeps* (literally 'first chief'), a title conferred on him by the Senate and renewed, at periods varying from five to ten years, till his death in 14 AD. Actual power was based on his position as Commander-in-Chief of the foreign provinces (*imperium*) and on the tribunician power (*tribunicia potestas*) in Rome itself. The tribunician power was originally designed as a democratic safeguard against the Senate, but Augustus and his successors used it as an effective means of wielding absolute power with some semblance of constitutional authority. It was not until 23 BC, however, that the position of Augustus, based on these powers at home and abroad, became rationalised. This constitutional change, one more stage in the progression from the Republic to the Empire, was reflected to some extent in the coins. The restoration of law and order, embodied in the nominal authority of the Senate, had its monetary parallel. The bronze coinage produced between 23 and 5 BC bore the letters S.C. (*Senatus consulto* – with the advice of the Senate). Coinage was in the hands of a college of moneyers as before, but by virtue of his tribunician power Augustus exercised close control over it.

Coins in gold or silver were minted at Rome between 19 and 12 BC, but although authority for them ostensibly derived, like the

97

a Augustus (27 BC–14 AD) obv: Augustus rev: equestrian figure; *b* denarius of Octavian obv: Octavian rev: Victory; *c* Augustus aureus (27 BC–14 AD) obv: laureate head of Augustus; *d* Augustus (27 BC–14 AD) stater of Antioch obv: Augustus rev: allegory of victory

a Tiberius (14–37 AD) obv: deified Augustus rev: seated figure of Livia;
b Tiberius (14–37 AD) denarius 'Tribute Penny' obv: Tiberias rev:
seated figure; *c* Tiberius (14–37 AD) assarion of Antioch

bronze issues, from the Senate, the pre-eminence of Augustus was
reflected in the use of his profile as a standard obverse type.
Following the emperor's visit to Gaul in 15–14 BC a mint was
established at Lugdunum (Lyons) and, according to contemporary
writers, the production of coins in precious metals was shortly
afterwards transferred to it. The coins of Lugdunum not only
extolled the virtues of Augustus himself but, more significantly,
gave prominence to members of his family, Gaius and Lucius
Caesar and Tiberius. In this we see a part of the process by which the

99

idea of a hereditary system was gradually promoted. During the last decade before Christ the minting of bronze coins was also transferred to Lugdunum and the mint at Rome closed down. The bronze coins of Lugdunum may be identified by their design showing the great altar which was a famous landmark in that city.

During the later years of his long life Augustus had carefully groomed his stepson Tiberius for high public office and though the hereditary principle was not by any means established Tiberius succeeded to the principate more or less automatically on the death of Augustus in 14 AD. In the reign of Tiberius (14–37 AD) the precious metal coins continued to be struck at Lugdunum while there was a revival of the Rome mint for bronze. The gold and silver coins were uniform in design, with an obverse showing a seated figure, veiled in mourning, and supposed to represent Livia, the mother of Tiberius, and widow of Augustus. The silver denarius of this series is commonly known as the Tribute Penny, since it would probably have been the coin used by Christ to illustrate his injunction 'to render unto Caesar the things that are Caesar's'.

Following a series of colonial rebellions against Rome the Lugdunum mint was partially closed down in 22 AD and henceforward the production of bronze coins was conducted in Rome. From this period also dates the interesting variety of coin types issued in the latter years of Tiberius's reign. Comparatively few of the coins actually portrayed Tiberius. His deified stepfather appeared on coins with the caption DIVUS AUGUSTUS PATER (Divine Father Augustus). Other designs portrayed Livia, Drusus (son of Tiberius) and even his grandchildren, Gemellus and Germanicus. Other coins, particularly in the bronze series, had allegorical subjects representing Piety, Clemency, Moderation and Justice. The Lugdunum mint was completely shut down by the great-grandson and successor of Tiberius, the notorious emperor Caligula. Henceforward the production of coins in both precious and base metals was carried on at Rome. Caligula grew up in an atmosphere of palace intrigue and was corrupted by the young Greek princes who resided there (as hostages for the good behaviour of the peoples of the eastern provinces). He suffered from mental weakness which supreme power merely accentuated. During his brief and unhappy reign his coins featured the deified Augustus and also his immediate predecessor Tiberius whom he attempted to have deified. No doubt influenced by contemporary Greek practices, he even tried to secure divine honours for himself. For the first time the emperor's portrait appeared on the humble bronze coins; hitherto only the gold or silver coins had been considered worthy of such portraiture. Aesthetically the coinage of Caligula bore signs of technical and artistic improvement. Portraiture was handled with a greater degree of sensitivity and more imaginative use was made of group composition.

The mad emperor Caligula was succeeded by his uncle, Claudius (son of Drusus and nephew of Tiberius). Claudius had led a life of comparative obscurity and probably because of his unprepossessing appearance, weak character and unattractive nature, never seemed a potential (and therefore dangerous) contender for the imperial throne. When the Praetorian Guard overthrew Caligula and murdered him it was with cynical irony that they selected the stuttering Claudius as his successor. Claudius reigned for thirteen years and attempted to rule as conscientiously as his limited abilities allowed, but he was very much under the domination of his wives, Messalina and Agrippina, and various cliques in court circles. The coinage of his reign finally broke with the tradition of alluding to the history of the moneyer's family and, instead, was used increasingly as a propaganda medium for extolling the virtues of the emperor and his relatives. The supposed merits in the emperor's character were proclaimed in allegory showing 'foresight', 'justice', 'mercy' and other statesmanlike qualities. Coins were used to familiarise the public with members of the imperial family. In Claudius's reign coins portrayed his father Drusus and his mother Antonia, while his second wife, Agrippina, became more frequently featured on coins towards the end of the reign. Agrippina persuaded her weak-willed husband to pass over his son Britannicus for the succession, and recognise her son by a previous marriage, Nero, as his heir instead. Several coins were struck in the time of Claudius depicting Nero and at least one of them was actually captioned PRINCEPS IUVENTUTIS (Prince of Youth) – the nearest equivalent in Roman times to Crown Prince or Heir Apparent.

a aureus of Claudius 46 AD   obv: Claudius   rev: triumphal arch symbolising the conquest of Britain; *b* Caligula (37–41 AD) obv: Caligula   rev: SPQR laureated; *c* Claudius (41–54 AD)   obv: Claudius rev: allegory of victory in Britain

Nero, the last emperor related by blood to Augustus, came to the throne in 54 AD and reigned for fourteen years. Agrippina, having secured his succession, sped things up by murdering Claudius. Nero in turn had his mother and his stepbrother Britannicus murdered. Against this background of savagery and corruption can be understood the excesses, the debauchery and criminality of the court of Nero, who instituted a reign of terror to eliminate all those, either corporately or individually, whom he

a Nero (54–68 AD) obv: Nero rev: allegory of Salus (security); *b* as of Nero 66 AD rev: altar of Peace; *c* Nero large bronze obv: Nero rev: winged figure of Rome

a

b

c

suspected of plotting his overthrow. A powerful rallying point for the opposition to Nero was the Senate which, during his reign, recovered something of its former position. This is reflected in the appearance of the formula EX S.C. (from the Senate in consultation) on the gold and silver coins of this period, as well as the bronze. In 63 AD, however, Nero succeeded in undermining the power of the Senate and in the latter years of his reign this formula is absent from his coins. The following year there was a partial reform of the coinage, the aureus being re-tariffed at 45 to the pound, while the denarius was reduced to a 96th part. Base metal coins, from the sestertius (2½ asses) to the quadrans (¼ as) were initially produced in a brass alloy known as orichalcum, but copper was subsequently reintroduced for the as. As well as promoting the public image of Nero and his family, the coins of this reign became increasingly commemorative and are of immense interest for their commentary on events of the period. In particular, coins were becoming highly pictorial, with representations of buildings, the new harbour at Ostia and other examples of grandiose public works inaugurated under Nero.

Discontent with the excesses of Nero's regime developed into open revolt in the provinces. Almost simultaneously rebellions broke out in Africa, in Gaul, Spain, the German frontier and in the East, all of which left their mark in Roman numismatics. Clodius Macer, the Legate of Numidia, whose revolt in Africa was the first against Nero, occupied Carthage where a series of denarii was struck in his name. These coins bore his portrait on the obverse and showed military standards on the reverse. Macer made no claim towards the principate and was content to establish a breakaway regime in Africa. Vindex in Gaul, however, was seriously opposed to Nero and all that he stood for. It is for this reason that the denarii and aurei minted, possibly at Vienne, under his authority, harked back to republican models, with allegorical types on both obverse and reverse. The abstract themes personified in these coins included the Genius of the Roman People and the Safety of Mankind.

The revolt of Vindex in the spring of 68 AD encouraged Galba in Spain to do likewise. Galba's denarii and aurei were probably struck at Tarraco and, like those of Vindex, went back to republican patterns for their subject-matter. Nero's portrait on the obverse of these coins was replaced by a profile representing the Genius of the Roman People, Good Fortune, Roma or Hispania. An interesting type, inspired by political motives, showed figures representing Gaul and Spain in harmony – a reference to the alliance of Vindex and Galba against Nero. In the early summer of 68 AD the legions of the West began their march on Rome where, on 9 June, the Praetorian Guard rose against their master Nero and compelled him to take his own life. The coins struck for Galba in that eventful year indicate most faithfully the development of events. Those struck in Spain bear only his title as *Imperator* (commander-in-chief). After Nero's death and Galba's recognition as emperor by the Senate, the title of Augustus was added to his coins. In July, when a senatorial commission went to Gaul to meet him, Galba added the title Caesar to his coins. After his installation at Rome, the letters PM began appearing on the coins as well, indicating Galba's assumption of the office of Pontifex Maximus (Chief Priest). The abbreviation TRP (*Tribunicia Potestas* – Tribunician Power) also appears on coins minted for Galba at Rome. Coins bearing Galba's portrait were produced at Lugdunum as well as at Rome. Allusive types and allegorical compositions accounted for the reverse designs of these issues.

Though Galba was widely acclaimed by both Senate and people he failed to win over the powerful Praetorian Guard who were disgruntled at his refusal to reward them for their support. In January 69 they staged a palace coup, murdered Galba, and proclaimed Otho emperor in his place. The legions in Gaul and the German frontier retaliated by acclaiming their commander-in-chief, Vitellius, as emperor, and invaded Italy to press his claim. Otho was defeated at Cremona in April and committed suicide. During his short reign Otho struck denarii and aurei at Rome bearing his curiously bewigged profile. Support for Vitellius had been growing even before the deposition of Galba and his coins first appeared at the end of 68. Allegorical subjects, such as the Loyalty of the Army, were featured on these coins, minted probably at Cologne. After the defeat of Otho and the assumption of the principate, Vitellius had coins struck at Rome. The earliest of these showed him bare-headed, with Imperator as his sole title. Later coins showed a laureated profile but no further elaboration in titles, though some referred to his period of office as Consul. Following his entry into Rome, however, new coins bearing the title Augustus were introduced. This series included bronze sestertii with finely engraved portraiture, in addition to the more usual gold and silver coins.

No sooner had Vitellius become installed at Rome than a fresh revolt occurred, this time in the eastern provinces which rose in support of Vespasian. Gold and silver coins bearing portraits of Vespasian (and occasionally his son Titus) were struck at Antioch (Syria) and an unknown mint in Illyricum (modern Yugoslavia). Following Vespasian's invasion of northern Italy in the summer of

a Galba (68–69 AD) obv: Galba rev: laureated inscription; *b* Otho (69 AD) obv: Otho wearing a wig rev: allegory of Peace

69 coins portraying him, and his sons Titus and Domitian, were struck at Lugdunum. In December Vespasian's troops entered Rome, Vitellius was put to death and the civil wars of the previous eighteen months came to an end with the surrender of the remnants of the Vitellian guard on 21 December. Four emperors had ruled in Rome in the space of one year and the rapid political changes of this period make the coins of 69 AD particularly interesting to the numismatist and historian.

With the death of Nero the Julio-Claudian line of emperors had come to an end. No return to a republican form of government was contemplated since it was realised that the imperial system was the one best suited to rule the vast conglomeration of territories which constituted the Roman world. The problems of the succession were all too evident in the bloody power struggles of 69. For this reason the establishment of a hereditary dynasty seemed all the more desirable. Vespasian, a man of comparatively humble birth who had risen to high military rank on merit alone, was quick to recognise this and therefore wasted no time in

a Vitellius (69 AD) obv: Vitellius rev: seated figure; *b* Vespasian denarius rev: Fortuna on prow; *c* Judaea Capta coin of 70 AD obv: Vespasian rev: allegory of vanquished Judaea; *d* Vespasian (69–79 AD) obv: Vespasian rev: temple; *e* Titus (79–81 AD) obv: deified Vespasian rev: allegory of Judeaea capta; *f* Julia obv: Julia rev: Apollo seated; *g* Domitian (81–96 AD) obv: Domitian rev: Minerva establishing the hereditary principle. During his reign of nine years he assiduously groomed his sons Titus and Domitian for the principate, and the high position in government which they enjoyed in their father's lifetime is reflected in the coins of Vespasian which often portrayed either one or both of his sons. On the death of Vespasian in 79 Titus assumed the title Augustus and Domitian became his heir. The coins issued under Titus featured his father and mother deified, his daughter Julia, and his brother Domitian as well as himself. He died in 81 and was succeeded by Domitian who reigned until 96. Bronze coins were produced at Lugdunum for a short time after his accession but from 82 onwards all the coins, in both base and precious metal, were struck at Rome. Most of the coins struck by Domitian have the goddess Minerva on the reverse, though a wide range of family portraits were shown on the obverse. In general the art of coin portraiture attained its peak in this period, the profiles being engraved with sensitivity and a warmth which has seldom been equalled, far less surpassed, since then.

Domitian, though popular with the masses, incurred the hostility of the patrician classes, and this alienation was his downfall. His paranoia, bordering on madness, led him to kill all those he feared would plot against him. In the end it was a freedman of his cousin Clemens (whom he had executed) who assassinated him in September 96. Fortunately for the Roman empire, the death of Domitian did not precipitate the civil war which had been experienced at the time of Nero's overthrow. The upper classes, through the medium of the Senate, secured the election of the elderly statesman and lawyer, Nerva, as emperor. Nerva's position was weakened by his relative unpopularity with the army but he silenced opposition by choosing as his heir Trajan, the army's most brilliant and popular general. In this way the system, whereby a successor was designated from among the ablest politicians, administrators and generals, was continued for almost a century, giving Rome a period of stability and efficient government. The adoptive emperors, as they are generally known, may be likened to republican presidents elected for life.

Nerva's principate was more or less in the nature of a caretaker government and his death in 98 led automatically to the elevation

of Trajan who had been virtual ruler of the empire in the previous two years. The coinage of Nerva's brief reign is, however, not without interest. The usual aurei and denarii were minted at Rome, with realistic profiles of Nerva on the obverse and allegorical types on the reverse. The bronze coinage, ranging from sestertius to quadrans, included a number of quasi-commemorative pieces, publicising the remission of taxes, the allocation of free corn and other measures taken to relieve the economic depression of the empire at this time.

Trajan ruled the empire for nineteen years – the longest reign since Augustus – and this period at the beginning of the second century witnessed Rome at the zenith of her power. Territorial expansion carried the boundaries of the empire to the Euphrates and the Caucasus in the east and to central Scotland in the north-west. Roman ambitions to incorporate the whole of Britain and to gain possession of the entire coastline of the Black Sea never materialised but they came near to realisation under Trajan. Lengthy campaigns were fought in what is now Romania, incorporated as the province of Dacia in 106. Ironically this area, one of the last to be brought under Roman control, has preserved in its name and in its language (Romance instead of Slavonic) the traditions of the Roman era far longer and more faithfully than many of the other dominions nearer Rome.

Despite the long colonial campaigns, involving the garrisoning of troops for years on end in remote outposts, little of this expansion had direct bearing on the coinage struck under Trajan, and the majority, if not all, of the coins were minted at Rome. Conversely, however, the military achievements of this reign received abundant publicity on coins which form a comprehensive record of victories, expeditions, campaigns and triumphs. At the same time the penchant for allegorical subjects was as strong as ever and symbolic designs representing Peace, Plenty and Prosperity are common. The portraiture on Trajan's coins was not as rugged as that of his predecessor. Among the members of the imperial family depicted were the emperor's deceased father, Trajan senior, his wife Plotina, his sister Marciana and his niece Matidia. On these coins the emperor's relatives are given the epithet *diva* or *divus* (divine). It seems paradoxical that an elective emperor, who might be of comparatively humble origins, should be worshipped as a god in his own lifetime and that this process of deification should even be extended to other members of his family. A practice initiated under Nerva and extended considerably by Trajan was the issue of 'restored' coins – reissues of coins current in previous reigns. Those of Nerva were only struck in bronze, but Trajan produced them in gold and silver and extended the range of types to include republican coins. These 'restored' coins may be easily distinguished from the originals by the inscription of Trajan's name and titles on the reverse, ending with the abbreviation REST (*restituit* – restored).

During the latter part of his reign Trajan groomed Hadrian as his successor, officially appointing him as heir shortly before his death. Numismatically as well as politically the succession of Hadrian marked the continuity of the regime. Even the idiosyncrasy of small heads and elongated busts which characterise the profiles on Trajan's coinage was carried over into Hadrian's reign. It was not long, however, before Hadrian began a process of rationalisation, cutting adrift those appendages of the empire which were difficult to administer efficiently. The remote eastern provinces of the Caucasus and Mesopotamia were evacuated. Instead Hadrian spent much of his time and energy travelling all over the empire, consolidating and strengthening it. It is not surprising, therefore, that many of the coins of this reign refer to the provinces and their development, pay tribute to various legions and their campaigns, or celebrate the various state visits of the

110

emperor to those far-off territories. The style of these coins was uniform, with a profile of Hadrian on the obverse and a pictorial design on the reverse. Generally speaking the subject of the reverse was allegorical, with a female figure indicating by means of dress or symbolism the appropriate province. The appearance of such figures before a sacrificial altar is usually taken to indicate the visit of the emperor to that province, a fact often borne out by the inscription. Coins celebrating military reviews have a stereotyped reverse showing the emperor on a dais addressing his soldiers.

After reigning for twenty years Hadrian nominated Lucius Aelius as his successor and he appears on coins struck in 137 with the title of Caesar. Aelius, however, predeceased Hadrian the following year and Hadrian himself only lived long enough to appoint Antoninus Pius as his heir. Coins portraying Antoninus, with a reverse type depicting an allegorical figure of Piety, appeared in the closing months of Hadrian's reign. Under Antoninus Pius the policies of Hadrian were continued. It was during these reigns, for example, that the frontiers of Roman Britain were clearly delineated, first by Hadrian's Wall (extending across present-day Cumberland and County Durham) and latterly by the Antonine Wall which guarded the isthmus between the Forth and Clyde in Scotland. Numismatically the trends initiated under Hadrian were also continued. Hadrian's wife, the empress Sabrina, produced her own coins in gold, silver and bronze, and this practice was not only continued by Faustina I, wife of Antoninus, but extended to his daughter, Faustina II. The simultaneous release of different coinages in such a long reign (Antoninus was on the throne from 138 to 161) makes the study of this period rather difficult, though the constant repetition of obverse and reverse types with minor variations has militated against the popularity of this series with collectors. Nevertheless the coins of this reign present a great deal of interest, especially those which are quasi-commemorative in character.

During this reign, for example, the ninth century of the foundation of Rome (148) was celebrated with great pomp and circumstance and inevitably the occasion was marked by a number of coins issued as much as four years prior to the event. Both

a Antoninus Pius; *b* Hadrian (117–38 AD) bronze sestertius; *c* Hadrian aureus (117–138 AD) obv: draped and cuirassed bust

precious and base metal coins of that period had frequent allusions to the legendary origins of Rome: Aeneas with Anchises and Ascanius fleeing from Troy, Mars and Rhea Silvia, Romulus and Remus. The reign of Antoninus was one of peace and tranquillity throughout the empire, and virtually the only campaign of note took place in Britain where the depredations of the Celtic tribes of Caledonia were checked by the Antonine Wall. This relatively minor campaign, however, was commemorated in a series of bronze sestertii showing the figure of Britannia seated on a rock and holding a staff and shield. This reverse type was repeated on asses of 154–5 and was, in fact, the prototype for the long series of Britannia reverses on the coins of Britain, begun under Charles II and continued down to the seven-sided 50 new pence coin of the present day.

The breakdown of the adoptive system began with Antoninus nominating Marcus Aurelius as his heir, and as early as 139–40 he was portrayed on coins, often on the reverse of pieces portraying the emperor. In 140, however he began issuing his own coins, bearing his profile and his titles as Caesar and 'Son of Pius', indicating that he had been formally adopted by Antoninus. In 145 the link between Marcus Aurelius and the emperor was strengthened by the marriage of Marcus to Faustina, daughter of Antoninus. She also was permitted the privilege of issuing her own coins, which began to appear some time after her marriage. These showed her profile on the obverse and various allegories such as Love, Modesty and Concord on the reverse.

On the death of Antoninus Pius in 161 Marcus Aurelius became emperor, a situation which seemed natural since Marcus had been closely associated with Antoninus throughout much of his reign. The policies inaugurated under Antoninus were continued by Marcus without change. During this reign, however, stagnation began to affect Roman civilisation and from then onwards the empire went into gradual decline. In the coins of this and succeeding reigns we begin to notice a more mechanical, stereotyped approach, especially in allegorical reverse types. Having attained high artistic standards at the beginning of the century it seemed that, if they could not be improved on, they should be imitated, but inevitably this lack of inspiration led to a deterioration in aesthetic quality. The coinage of this reign was as prolific as that of the preceding one. In addition to the series of the emperor himself, coins were struck for his wife Faustina II. A novel feature of this reign, however, was the appointment of a sort of co-emperor instead of nominating an heir. During the early years of this reign Lucius Verus acted as 'associate emperor' and both he and his wife Lucilla produced their own coins. In the latter half of the reign, following the death of Lucius in 169, the emperor's own son, Commodus, was brought into the limelight, being nominated Caesar in 172, and Augustus in 177, with the privilege of striking his own coins.

By contrast with the tranquillity of the previous reign, the period of Marcus Aurelius was continually disturbed by revolts, frontier wars and disturbances, the principal causes of trouble being the Parthians in the eastern provinces and the Germanic tribes north of the Danube. The Parthian wars and the Danubian campaigns found copious record on the coins of Marcus and Lucius and the latter were strongly featured on the coins of Commodus. The successful outcome of these expeditions was

113

marked by series of Victory coins which record the triumphal processions held in Rome at the conclusion of each campaign.

Commodus, son of Marcus Aurelius and grandson of Antoninus Pius, had little of the statesmanlike qualities of his predecessors and, though he reigned for twelve years, it soon became apparent that the hereditary system was not as effective as the adoptive system for assuring good government from Rome. The chaos and corruption prevalent in this period find little reflection in the coins of Commodus, except in a rather negative sense. The revolt of the Praetorian Guard in 184 was countered by a series of propaganda coins promoting the loyalty of the armed services. These pieces had allegorical reverses captioned 'Loyalty of the Armies' or 'Harmony of the Soldiery'. Most of the coins of this reign follow the pattern set under previous rulers. One novelty, however, was the predilection of Commodus for Greek or Oriental religious cults and this found expression on some of his coins. In particular Commodus venerated the Greek hero Hercules and, like Alexander the Great five hundred years earlier, alluded to Hercules on his coins. The coins showing Commodus in the lion-skin head-dress connected with Hercules are not unlike the tetradrachms of the Alexandrian empire. Coins were struck for a short period by the empress Crispina and a series dedicated to the deified Marcus Aurelius also appeared early in this reign.

On New Year's Eve 192 the Antonine dynasty came to an abrupt end with the murder of Commodus. Political negligence and personal debauchery alienated the conservative upper and middle classes, though Commodus, like Nero, had curried favour with the masses by his policy of 'bread and circuses'. Like the downfall of Nero, the assassination of Commodus brought a period of instability to the empire with no fewer than five emperors in 193 – Pertinax, Didius Julianus, Pescennius Niger, Clodius Albinus and Septimius Severus. Pertinax, prefect of the city of Rome, was an immediate stop-gap choice whose brief reign was terminated by murder at the hands of the Praetorian Guard. His coins, struck at Rome, featured his bust on the obverse and various allegorical reverse designs including the Goddess of Good Advice. Janus, a deity specially connected with the New Year (from his name is derived January) was a particularly appropriate subject since the reign of Pertinax began on New Year's Day.

Didius Julianus secured the succession to Pertinax with bribes. Because of this incident it was said that the Praetorian Guard had sold the imperial throne to the highest bidder. Didius did not live long to enjoy the principate, being deposed and put to death in June following the successful invasion of Italy by the armies of Septimius Severus, governor of Pannonia (now north-western Yugoslavia). The coinage of this brief reign includes obverse types with the bombastic title RECTOR ORBIS (ruler of the world). Both his wife Manlia Scantilla and his daughter Didian Clara struck their own coins, but these are exceedingly rare.

The three other contenders for the throne were governors of provinces – Pescennius Niger in Syria, Clodius Albinus in Britain and Septimius Severus in Pannonia. Of these the third succeeded by defeating the first in battle and adopting the second as his heir. Pescennius is remembered by some crudely struck aurei and denarii produced at Antioch, while Clodius Albinus (in his role of Caesar) had coins issued in his name at Rome in 193–5. In 195, however, he quarrelled with Septimius and fled to Gaul where he had himself proclaimed Augustus. Coins bearing his name with this title were minted at Lugdunum in 196. His breakaway regime was brought to an end the following February when he was defeated in battle near Lugdunum.

By contrast with the rare coinages of the ephemeral emperors the coins struck in the reign of Septimius Severus were prolific and profuse in their variety. First of all, Severus reigned for a comparatively long time, from 193 to 211. Secondly, coins were struck for him not only at Rome but in provincial mints at Alexandria (Egypt), Emesa (Syria) and Laodicea (Greece). Thirdly, series of coins were produced not only for the emperor, but also for his wife Julia Domna, his two sons Caracalla and Geta, and even for Caracalla's wife Plautilla. That the sons of Severus were both associated with him in the government of the empire in the latter part of his reign is borne out by the title Augustus found on many of their coins.

With the appearance of the Severan emperors the principate entered a new phase of autocracy and military dictatorship. Dependence on the army for the continuance of their power is

115

a denarius Septimius Severus; *b* Plautilla denarius 202 AD rev: Concordia

a

b

reflected in the coins devoted to extolling the prowess of the various legions. The coins struck at Alexandria and Emesa, being essentially military issues for the payment of the troops engaged in the campaign of 193–5 against Pescennius Niger, also had a strong military bias in their choice of reverse designs, although the age-old traditions of eastern numismatics had a strong influence on the fabric and style of these coins. Attempts by Septimius Severus to lend an air of legitimacy to his rule are seen in those coins of Septimius which include the surname Pius and those of Caracalla suffixed Antoninus. Coins were thus employed as a means towards associating the regime more closely with its predecessors.

On the death of Severus his sons, both designated Augustus in his lifetime, returned from campaigns abroad to Rome where they ruled as joint emperors. This condominium lasted for a few months till Caracalla simplified matters by murdering his brother. The coins issued in their joint names were similar to the last issues of Septimius Severus, the sole means of identification being in the

a Julia Domna aureus 202 AD rev: Mars; *b* denarius Severus Alexander
222–235 AD rev: Mars

a

b

reverse inscription where the numbering of the tribunician power
differs from the preceding series. More distinctive were the coins
dedicated to the deified Septimius, showing his funeral pyre.
Caracalla reigned on his own for five years before he, in turn, was
despatched in time-honoured fashion by the Praetorian Guard.
The coins of his reign are of great interest. The evolution of his
title inscribed on these coins reflected the chain of events in this
period. Like his father before him he used the title Britannicus, an
allusion to their campaigns in that remote province (Severus died
at York). Later coins had the epithet *Felix* (lucky) substituted and
then, after his successful campaign against the Germans, he added
the title Germanicus to his coins. In 212 the privileges of Roman
citizenship were extended to everyone of free birth resident in the
empire. Oddly enough, this dramatic constitutional change found
no expression on the coins of that year, though the Liberty reverse
type popular on coins of 213 may allude to it. A new coin, the
double-denarius, was introduced in 214. Apart from the larger size
this coin is recognisable by the profile of the emperor which was
shown with a radiate (sun's rays) crown, instead of a crown of
laurel leaves. A series of coins including double-denarii were
minted for the dowager empress Julia Domna, with various
allegorical reverse types including the moon-goddess whom she
seems to have specially venerated.

Caracalla was succeeded briefly by the Praetorian prefect
Macrinus who, after reigning for a year, was defeated by
Elagabalus, grandson of Julia Maesa (sister of Julia Domna), and
put to death. Macrinus attempted to legitimise his rule by
adopting the surnames of both Severan and Antonine dynasties. A
curious feature of his coins was the use of two portraits, one of a

117

youngish man with a short beard, the other of an older man with a longer beard. It has been suggested quite plausibly that the earlier type was a modification of the profile used on coins of Caracalla and was used to make the transition from one reign to the next smoother. Having established his imperial authority Macrinus may have adopted a more realistic profile. His successor Elagabalus adopted for his coins the style and title of Marcus Aurelius Antoninus, referring to his supposed connections with the Antonine dynasty. The reign of Elagabalus, one of the worst and most profligate since the time of Nero, was a mercifully short one, since he was deposed by his cousin Severus Alexander in 222. Elagabalus was preoccupied with sun-worship (alluded to on several coins showing him as high priest of the sun cult) and also tried to promote the worship of himself. The horn of Ammon, similar to the device on the profile of Alexander the Great (on coins of Lysimachus) appeared on the obverse portraits of Elagabalus, the major difference between these denarii and the earlier tetradrachms being that the horn of deification appeared on coins in the lifetime of Elagabalus. Prolific coinage was struck in this short reign not only for the emperor but also for his grandmother Julia Maesia, his mother Julia Soaemias, and his three wives Julia Paula, Aquilia Severa and Annia Faustina.

Julia Maesia persuaded Elagabalus to adopt his cousin Alexander as his heir and then promptly engineered his removal. His coins were similar in appearance to those of Elagabalus in the early period but gradually a more realistic portrait emerged. Allegorical reverse types vied with quasi-commemorative designs marking the progress of campaigns against the Germans and the Parthians which dominated this reign. Internal affairs were also highlighted with coin types celebrating the restoration or rebuilding of such Roman landmarks as the Colosseum and the Nymphaceum. Coinage was also struck by his mother Julia Marnaea and his wife Orbiana. The coins of the latter are rare, mainly on account of their ephemeral nature, since Orbiana was banished after two turbulent years of marriage. During the last seven years of his reign Alexander was very much under his mother's influence, with detrimental effect on the principate. While on a military expedition against the Germans in 235 Alexander and his mother were murdered by mutinous troops who proclaimed their general Maximius as emperor instead. This return to anarchy ushered in the stormy era of the military emperors. A series of revolts broke out in 238, culminating in the deposition of Maximius. In that year alone there were no fewer than six emperors. In North Africa Gordian I and his son Gordian II ruled for a few short weeks, the Senate elected Balbinus and Pupienus as joint emperors in April, and following their murder by the Praetorian Guard in July their deputy was elevated to the throne as Gordian III. Coins were struck at Rome for all of these rulers but apart from the titles shown in the inscriptions there is little to distinguish these issues, though the coin-engravers must have worked overtime to produce reasonably good likenesses preserving the different characters of these emperors.

Gordian III ruled for the comparatively lengthy period of six years before his assassination while campaigning in the eastern provinces and Persia. During this period the double-denarius became the principal coin and the denarius was comparatively rarely issued. This practice was continued and elaborated during the reign of his successor. Gordian was succeeded by joint emperors, Philip father and son, both of whom struck coins in the period from 244 to 249. The main numismatic interest of this reign lies in the coins of 248 commemorating the thousandth anniversary of the foundation of Rome. These commemorative coins, featuring animals on the reverse, bore numerals from I to VI, indicating in which of the six mint workshops they had been struck. In addition, code letters in the Greek alphabet were employed on other coins and from these numismatists have been able to deduce the division of labour between the workshops in the production of coins for the two emperors and the empress Octacilia Severa.

The short reign of Trajan Decius (249–51), who rebelled against the Philips and successfully invaded Italy, was marked by prolific issues not only for Trajan but for his wife and his two sons. The chief interest of this period, numismatically speaking, is in the introduction of a new bronze coin, the double sestertius. In addition to the coins struck at Rome and the eastern mint of Antioch, it was during this reign that a mint was established at

Gallienus antoninianus *c.* 266 AD

Mediolanum (Milan). It is thought that this mint was set up to produce coins for the payment of the troops stationed in the great plains of northern Italy to meet the threat of invasion from the tribes of northern and eastern Europe who had become more active in the middle of the third century. The menace of the Goths, Huns and Vandals beset the empire from this time onwards. In 251 Trajan and his son Etruscus were in fact killed in battle during the campaign against these barbarians. The younger son, Hostilian, died of the plague soon afterwards and the principate then devolved on Trebonianus Gallus who ruled jointly with his son Volusian. Coins were struck for both of them over the ensuing two years at all three mints. Inflation caused by the lengthy foreign wars began to make itself felt. The double sestertius disappeared and the double denarius shrank in size and value to the equivalent of the former denarius. Ironically it was in his former province of Moesia that Trebonianus was first opposed by his successor as governor. Aemilian was proclaimed emperor there by his troops, who advanced into Italy and defeated Trebonianus. Aemilian ruled for barely three months before he was, in turn, deposed by Valerian. During his brief reign, however, coins were struck at Rome for Aemilian and his wife Cornelia and these are comparatively rare.

Valerian appointed his son Gallienus as co-emperor and together they reigned for six years. In an attempt to stave off the external menace of the barbarians the empire was partitioned between these rulers in 259. In that year, however, Valerian was captured by the Sassanians who had invaded the eastern provinces and though Gallienus continued to rule in the west till 268, the demoralising effect of the loss of the eastern provinces led to the temporary secession of Gaul where a separate empire existed from 259 to 274. The upheavals of this period witnessed coins struck under the joint rule of Valerian and Gallienus, under Gallienus alone and for the empress Salonina. Pretenders to the throne in Syria (Macrian and Quietus) and Dacia (Regalian) also produced coins to back up their claims in 259. The only successful revolt that year was in Gaul, where Postumus, governor of the provinces on the German frontier, established himself as emperor in Gaul, Germany and Britain. Postumus and Gallienus ruled their respective empires till 268. In that year Gallienus was murdered while besieging Milan (held by the Goths), while Postumus was killed while laying siege to Mainz where a military revolt under Laelian was in progress. Postumus was briefly followed by Marius before he, too, was eliminated in favour of Victorinus, who ruled for less than two years. The last of the Gallic emperors was Tetricius who reigned from 270 to 274 before surrendering his empire to Rome. Gallienus was succeeded at Rome by Claudius II in 268. Two years later Claudius died of the plague and was followed by his brother Quintillus for a few brief months. Aurelian, who came to the throne in 270, fared rather better. Although he ruled for only four years he succeeded in recovering the western provinces and also won back most of the eastern provinces, though Dacia was abandoned.

The coinage of the fifteen years between the capture of Valerian and the consolidation of the empire reflects the turbulence of the period. Apart from the large number of temporary issues made by ephemeral rulers and usurpers, the almost continuous state of war, with many campaigns being fought on Roman soil, was characterised by the numerous coins with a military theme. The economic straits of the empire at this time led to a rapid debasement of the coinage. Not only had the size of the double-denarius shrunk, so that it approximated to the former denarius in weight, but increasing amounts of copper were alloyed with the silver until the base metal predominated. These coins may more properly be termed billon, the name given to a copper-silver alloy. Gold coins continued to appear, but since the intrinsic value of the metal was real, the nominal value of these aurei, in relation to the denarii, varied considerably. Stylistically the coins of this period present a measure of uniformity, marked by a stagnation in artistic

a antoninianus third century; *b* Maximian (286–305 AD) follis obv: Maximian rev: Moneta

originality and technical execution. The only series of note were the radiate profile coins of Tetricius, partly on account of the fact that they are comparatively plentiful, and partly because they provided the popular model for the barbarous imitations used by the Goths and other northern nations when they began issuing their own coins.

The political and economic consolidation of the empire begun under Aurelius and continued down to the end of the century had its effects on the coinage of Rome. The coinage was reformed: aurei were struck in weight standards similar to those in operation before the disintegration of the empire in 259, and double-denarii were struck in billon of a higher silver content. The number of reverse types was decreased and some attempt at standardisation of coin design was made, not only for the mint at Rome but for the mints which existed at Antioch, Lugdunum and a recently established mint in the Balkan town of Serdica (modern Sofia). A military coup overthrew Aurelian in 274 and there was something of a hiatus before the Senate appointed the elder statesman Tacitus to the principate. He died a few months later and was succeeded by his brother Florian who, in turn, reigned briefly

a Carausius (286–293 AD) denarius obv: Carausius rev: allegory of
peace; *b* Carausius denarius obv: Carausius rev: galley; *c* Carausius
antoninianus of the London mint

before being ousted by Probus who commanded the eastern
provinces recently regained. Probus managed to hang on to his
throne for the comparatively lengthy period of six years (276–82).
Under Probus the variety of reverse types was increased again,
while a complex system of codes and mintmarks added considerably to the numismatic interest of this reign.

a Allectus denarius obv: Emperor rev: galley; *b* Allectus (293–296 AD)
antoninianus obv: Allectus rev: Laetitia; *c* Antoninianus of Allectus

Probus was put to death by mutinous troops who elected their
commander, Carus, as emperor. Carus ruled jointly with his sons
Carinus and Numerian, coins being struck at Rome, Antioch and
Lugdunum for all three. Following the deaths of Carus and
Numerian in 284, Diocletian was appointed co-emperor, elimi-
nating Carinus the following year. Simultaneously there was a

brief revolt in Pannonia where a pretender to the throne, Julian, produced his own coins at Siscia. The coinage of the family of Carus is relatively undistinguished and few distinctive reverse types were used. Diocletian, however, proved to be an innovator in both political and numismatic matters and the reforms which he instituted in both fields had a marked effect on the later history of the Roman empire.

Between 284 and 295 Diocletian ruled with a succession of co-emperors, with whom he divided the administrative control of the empire. Maximian was appointed Augustus and given control of the western provinces, with Galerius as his Caesar, or deputy. Diocletian ruled the remaining provinces with Constantius Chlorus. Coins were struck for all four rulers and a greater number of mints was in operation than at any time previously. In addition to Rome, Antioch and Ludgunum, there were mints at Siscia, Trier (Augusta Treviorum) and Heraclea in Thrace. Serdica, which had ceased to mint coins in the reign of Probus, was not revived. The majority of the coins produced were the small billon denarii known as *antoniniani,* but it is significant that a wide variety of aurei were also struck in different weights, heralding the important monetary reforms which were instituted in 295.

To this period belongs the breakaway regime known as the British empire, established in 286 by Carausius and controlling the territory of Britain in what is now England, with part of Wales and a portion of north-western France. Carausius reigned in defiance of central authority at Rome until his murder in 293. In that year the Continental territory adhering to the British empire was recaptured by Rome. Carausius was succeeded by Allectus who gradually brought his empire back under the domination of Rome. Distinctive coins on Roman models were produced by mints at London and Camulodunum (Colchester) and also, for a time, at Boulogne. A conciliatory attitude towards the authority of Rome is reflected in the predominant reverse type featuring an allegory of Peace. Some of the later coins of Carausius bore the names of Diocletian and Maximian, recognising their nominal overlordship, while the curious abbreviation for *Augusti,* AVGGG, is taken to indicate the existence of not one but three emperors.

9 the later empire
295-476 AD

The year 295-6 was an outstanding landmark in the history of the Roman empire. The secessionist regime in Britain was brought to an end and the central authority of Rome was consolidated and reinforced by a number of political reforms, the most important of these being the establishment of a tetrarchy (a Greek word meaning four-fold rule) consisting of Diocletian, Maximian, Constantius and Galerius. After a decade both Diocletian and Maximian stepped down, their deputies were promoted to Augusti and new Caesars, Severus and Maximinus, were appointed. When Constantius Chlorus died in 306 Severus was promoted to fill the vacancy and Constantine, son of Constantius, was appointed Caesar. Although the tetrarchy system proved in the end to be unworkable, and was replaced in 313-14 by the rule of one Augustus, it was a bold measure which, under different circumstances, might have been more successful.

In monetary matters Diocletian was more successful and the reforms he wrought had a more permanent effect. The basis of these reforms was the introduction of an aureus struck at 60 to the pound and a denarius struck at 96 to the pound. In addition there was a large bronze coin with a silver wash known as a follis and base metal coins which are thought to have been equal in value to the old double denarius and denarius respectively. On account of the inflation of the Roman economy, however, both gold and silver coins tended to disappear rapidly from circulation and they were minted less and less frequently as time went by. Instead the follis

a Constantine the Great (306–337 AD) follis obv: Constantine
rev: Genius; *b* Constantine the Great reduced follis obv: Constantine
rev: Sol (sun-god)

and the other base metal coins were produced in greater quantity.
The increasing popularity of the follis is shown by the fact that,
whereas under the first tetrarchy one standard reverse was used,
showing the Spirit of the Roman People, in subsequent tetrarchies
a wide variety of reverse types was employed. The variety of coin
types increased enormously after 295, as a result of new mints
established at Ticinum and Aquileia in northern Italy, Thes-
salonica (Salonika) in Thrace, Carthage in North Africa and
Nicomedia in Asia. In addition the mints at Alexandria and
Serdica were revived and the mint at London, established by the
erstwhile British empire, continued to operate. Rome, Lugdunum,
Antioch, Siscia and Heraclea continued to mint coins as before.
Although some attempt at uniformity of design was attempted the
regional mints inevitably produced their own local variants, and
the folles of the early fourth century present a very complicated
period in Roman numismatics.

The situation was further complicated by the civil wars which

127

rent the Empire after Maximian tried to stage a comeback in 306. His son Maxentius was proclaimed Augustus at Rome and coins in his name were subsequently struck there and at several other mints. Though Severus was eliminated on the battlefield in 307 Maximian had Constantine elevated to Augustus and a new co-emperor, Licinius, was appointed to rule the eastern provinces. By the end of the first decade of the century there were no fewer than six Augusti ruling the empire. In the ensuing three years coins were struck for Maxentius in Italy, for Constantine in Britain and Gaul, and for Galerius, Maximinus and Licinius in the Balkans and the East. The British and Gallic mints also struck coins for Maximian for a brief period before his deposition in 310. In addition occasional issues from the eastern mints bore the name of Constantine, though the reciprocal was never practised by the western mints. During this period Maxentius closed the Carthage mint and transferred it to Ostia, the seaport of Rome, which began striking coins in 308.

The civil wars of this period became crystallized into two main power struggles, in the west between Constantine and Maxentius and in the east between Licinius and Maximinus. Constantine defeated his rival in 312 and the following year Licinius secured the overthrow of Maximinus. Constantine then turned on Licinius whom he drove out of the Balkans in 314. Licinius managed to retain command of Thrace and the Asiatic provinces till 324 when Constantine finally ousted him and re-united the empire under one ruler. Constantine celebrated his victory by founding a new capital city on the Bosphorus on the site of the old Byzantium and named it Constantinople. A mint was established there the following year and thus was begun an era in numismatics which continued for more than eleven centuries till the capture of the city by the Turks in 1453.

The chief innovation in the coinage of this reign was the introduction of the solidus, a gold coin smaller than the aureus and struck at 72 to the pound. The aureus continued to appear for some years in the eastern provinces but disappeared in 325. The solidus was the ancestor of a large family of coins found in medieval and modern European coinage – the soldo, sol or sou – and was preserved in the British monetary system as the abbrevia-

a Constantine small bronze; *b* Crispus small bronze; *c* Constantine I
c. 330 AD small bronze

tion 's' used to denote shillings in financial notation. Silver coins
were not minted to any extent in the reign of Constantine or his
immediate successors, and even the bronze coins of this period
dwindled steadily in size and weight. The coin types of this period
ranged from the usual allegorical reverses to elaborate motifs
commemorating important victories both in the civil wars and
against the barbarians of northern Europe. The enormous range
of coin series produced during the tetrarchies, for the Augusti, the
Caesars and their families, set the trend for the prolific issues
struck by the numerous relations of Constantine: his four sons

Crispus, Constantine II, Constantius II, and Constans, his nephews Dalmatius and Hannibalian, his mother Helena and step-mother Theodora, and his wife Fausta. The greatest variety and interest lies in the gold coins of this period. The bronze, dwindling in size and importance, tended to be fairly uniform in design, the most popular reverse type being the camp-gate.

Constantine's eldest son Crispus and his wife Fausta conspired against him in 326, but paid the supreme penalty for their treachery. On Constantine's death in 337 his three remaining sons ruled as joint Augusti, dividing responsibility for the provinces among them. Coins, either gold or small bronze, were struck at Rome, Constantinople and other mints in the joint names of the three brothers. The most frequent themes found on these coins concerned victory and the prowess of the army, reflecting the dependence of the government on military forces for the maintenance of rule within the empire and protection from the barbarians without. During the reign of Constantine the Great, Christianity made great headway in the empire, leading to the conversion of Helena and the emperor himself. This religious revolution, however, found no expression on the coins of this reign, although a reverse type found on solidi bears a curious portrait of Constantine gazing upwards – perhaps an allusion to the vision of the Cross which appeared in the sky on the eve of the battle in which he defeated Maxentius. Coins struck by his sons portray Constantine the Great with the customary caption referring to his deification, at variance with Christian practice.

In the middle of the fourth century larger bronze coins began to appear, with quasi-commemorative subjects. These large pieces are regarded as the forerunners of the commemorative medals which appeared in Renaissance Italy and became very popular all over western Europe in the fifteenth century. These commemorative coins had a wide variety of reverse designs, some obvious and others obscure. Of the former the most celebrated are those which marked the eleven hundredth anniversary of the foundation of Rome, in 348. Two years later Constans was ousted in the western provinces by Magnentius whose coins were struck in Gaul and Italy both for himself and for his brother Decentius as Caesar. The chief claim of Magnentius to numismatic fame is his bronze coinage bearing the XP (chi-rho) monogram of Christ. At the time of the defeat of Constans in 350 Constantine's nephew ruled for a few weeks as Augustus in Rome – just long enough for coins to be minted in his name. Coins also appeared at the Balkan mints for the brief rule of the usurper Vetranio in that critical year. Over the ensuing two years, however, Constantius gradually overthrew both Vetranio and Magnentius and by the beginning of 353 had regained control of Gaul and the Balkans. To this period belong the prolific issues of solidi featuring the Glory of the Republic on the reverse, symbolised by female figures representing Rome and Constantinople holding a shield bearing reference to the vows connected with the thirtieth anniversary of Constantine's reign.

From 351 to 354 Constantius Gallus, cousin of Constantius, acted as his Caesar or deputy but in the latter year he was removed from office and put to death, being succeeded by his half-brother, Julian. Joint issues of coins reflected these changes, first in the names of Constantius and Gallus and then for Constantius and Julian. The latter was acclaimed as Augustus by his armies in 360 and although Constantius objected to this, his death the following year forestalled the inevitable clash. Coins were minted in the western provinces for Julian as emperor from 360 until his death in 363 while campaigning in the east. New coins introduced in this period were the silver *miliarensium* and the smaller *siliqua*. Shortly before his death Julian reformed the bronze coinage with a large bronze coin showing a bull on the reverse. Julian's successor, Jovian, died after a few months' rule and is remembered mainly for his gold coins with the common 'Safety of the Republic' reverse and his large bronzes bearing the allegory of Roman victory.

The death of Jovian in 364 and the appointment of Valentinian as Augustus ushered in a new dynasty of emperors. Valentinian divided responsibility for the empire with his brother Valens, controlling the western and eastern provinces respectively. In this period there was something of a revival in the use of silver and increasingly frequent issues of coins in this metal were made. The coins found in this period were the solidus or aureus and half aureus in gold, the miliarensium and the siliqua in silver, and the

a Valentinian (364–378 AD) solidus of Trier   obv: Valentinian   rev: Valens and Valentinian; *b* Valens (364–378) solidus of Antioch   obv: Valens   rev: Rome and Constantinople holding a shield; *c* Theodosius I (379–395) solidus   obv: Theodosius   rev: allegory of Constantinople

various small bronze coins, the large bronze disappearing from the series soon after the commencement of the reign. The previous tendency towards commemorative or allusive reverse types was reversed and in its place there was a return to the routine allegorical types. To the coins of the joint emperors in this period may be added the group minted for the usurper Procopius in 365-6 (from the eastern mints) and the coins of Gratian, son of

a Magnus Maximus (383–388) gold solidus of the London mint; *b* Arcadius (383–408) solidus of Constantinople obv: Arcadius rev: allegory of Constantinople; *c* Constantine III (407–411) solidus

a

b

c

Valentinian, who became co-emperor in 367. Valentinian I died in 375 and his younger son Valentinian II was raised to the principate. In 387 Valens died and was replaced by Theodosius with control of the eastern provinces. During this period the same sort of allegorical design was continued, with rather more variety in the silver and base metal coins than had hitherto been the case.

133

The commonest reverse types on the gold coins of this period were Victory (western mints) and Concordia AUGGG (harmony of the three Augusti). The Harmony of the Emperors was a popular theme on most of the denominations struck at Constantinople in the early years of Theodosius's reign.

Following the uprising of Magnus Maximus in Britain and Gaul, and his subsequent defeat of Gratian in 386, he was recognised as emperor by Valentinian and Theodosius. Maximus appointed his son Victor as his co-emperor, while Theodosius proclaimed his son Arcadius, so once again the Roman empire had no fewer than five Augusti at the same time. The overweening ambition of Maximus proved his downfall. In 387 he invaded Italy but was defeated and killed the following year and Victor suffered the same fate soon aferwards. The short-lived reign of Maximus and Victor is recorded in the coinage of the London mint which flourished briefly in this period. Fewer gold coins were minted in the empire at this time, the eastern mints alone producing any sizeable quantity of solidi. On the other hand the western mints produced more silver coins and greater use was made of the large bronze coins than previously.

With the elimination of Maximus and Victor the division of the empire began to take shape more clearly. Valentinian II continued to rule the west till his murder in 392, when he was succeeded by Eugenius. Theodosius refused to recognise Eugenius whom he defeated in battle two years later and replaced by his younger son Honorius. During this period the reverse types of Victory, Concord, the Glory of the Romans and the Security of the Republic continued as the main reverse types.

When Theodosius died in 395 his sons divided responsibility for the administration of the empire as before, Honorius ruling the western provinces and Arcadius governing the east. The practice of dividing administrative responsibility was an old-established one but instead of continuing, as before, to rule in their joint names, the two emperors began to govern their respective territories as separate entities. The division of the Roman empire into East and West was not accomplished overnight with dramatic suddenness. It developed gradually, as political exigencies and military necessity demanded. Over the ensuing generations the

Western empire was subject increasingly to barbarian onslaught and was eventually overrun, but some semblance of the old order remained in the Eastern empire which, although it shrank in area and importance with the passage of time, continued to exist in an attenuated form for a further thousand years.

Rome, the imperial city which had given the empire its name, dwindled rapidly in importance in the later years of the fourth century, its place being taken by Constantinople. Before the century was out Rome had even ceased to be the administrative capital of the West, the imperial court having moved to Ravenna in AD 395. As befitted the capital, a new mint was established in Ravenna which rapidly gained in importance, though coins continued to be produced at Rome, Trier, and other western mints. In the early years of the fifth century the western mints continued to strike coins in the names of both Arcadius and Honorius but only the Ravenna mint struck coins for Theodosius II, son of Arcadius who became joint emperor in 402. Five years later the usurper Constantine III was proclaimed emperor by his troops in Britain and invaded the Continent, eventually gaining control of most of Gaul. Gold solidi in his name were struck at the Gallic mints till his death in 411. Constantine III was succeeded by Jovinus, while other short-lived uprisings were headed by Maximus in Spain and Priscus Attalus in Rome itself. After the death of Honorius in 423 Johannes reigned briefly at Ravenna. All of these emperors, pretenders to the throne, and their Caesars struck coins at one or several of the mints located in the western provinces. Although artistically poor and stylistically monotonous these coins reflect the complex politics of the Western empire and the disorder and anarchy into which it had fallen. By contrast the coinage of the Eastern empire was more uniform and less complicated with mints operating only at Salonika and Constantinople as far as gold and silver were concerned (though a wider variety resulted from the production of bronze coins at numerous provincial mints).

The chaos of the early years of the fifth century gave way to a period of strong government and relative tranquillity in the West. Valentinian III reigned from 425 to 455 – the longest reign since the time of the first Augustus (though, in the East, Theodosius ruled from 402 to 450). During this period, however, the number of mints producing coins declined, as did also the output of different coins. After 410 Rome abandoned Britain to the barbarians and soon Gaul and the German border areas were evacuated. By the middle of the century the Western empire had withdrawn into Italy, whence it had expanded seven centuries earlier. This drastic contraction in the face of barbarian aggression was marked by the disappearance of the Gallic mints. Apart from a few issues of solidi at Ravenna the majority of coins in this period were struck at Rome. These included the tremissis, a small gold coin equal to one third of a solidus, the silver siliqua and low-denomination bronze pieces. Coins were struck not only for Valentinian III but for his mother Galla Placidia, his wife Eudoxia and his sister Honoria. Coins in the name of Valentinian III continued to be minted at Constantinople, maintaining the pretence of imperial solidarity, but by the middle of the century the two areas were practically separate countries.

After Valentinian's death there was again a period of anarchy marked by a spate of ephemeral rulers: Petronius Maximus (455), Avitus (455-6), Majorian (457-61), Libius Severus (461-5), Anthemius (467-72), Olybrius (472), Glycerius (473-4), Julius Nepos (474-5) and Romulus Augustus (475-6). The coinage of these emperors was undistinguished and monotonous, being produced in Rome, Ravenna and Milan (and for a brief period at Arles in Gaul). Apart from stereotyped solidi in patterns similar to those of previous reigns the coins of this twilight period consisted of a few silver siliquae with the chi-rho monogram of Christianity on the reverse. The small bronze coins of this period borrowed from the East the practice of placing the emperor's monogram on the reverse, in place of the allegorical or quasi-historical subjects of former times. The last Roman emperor in the West, ironically bearing the name of Rome's founder, was overthrown by the Ostrogoths in 476 and Italy was overrun by the barbarians. Barbarous coins were struck at Rome by Theodoric the Ostrogothic king with reverse types depicting a figure of Rome captioned INVICTA ROMA (Unconquered Rome), but nevertheless Rome, its culture and its coinage in the classical sense had come to an end.

bibliography

Babelon, E. *Traité des Monnaies Grecques et Romaines* Paris, 1901

Babelon, Jean *Great Coins and Medals* Thames and Hudson, London, 1959

British Museum *Catalogues of Greek Coins*, 29 vols, London, 1873–1927

A Guide to the Principal Coins of the Greeks London, 1932

Carson, R. A. G. *Coins: Ancient, Medieval & Modern* Hutchinson, London, 1962

Davis, Norman *Greek Coins and Cities* Spink, London, 1967

Gardner, Percy *The Types of Greek Coins* Cambridge University Press, 1883

Grueber, Harold A. *Roman Republican Coins* London, 1874

History of Ancient Coinage Clarendon Press, Oxford, 1918

Head, Barclay V. *Historia Numorum* Clarendon Press, Oxford

Hill, Sir George F. *Handbook of Greek and Roman Coins* London, 1899

Historical Greek Coins Constable, London, 1906

Historical Roman Coins Constable, London, 1909

Laing, Lloyd R. *Coins in Archaeology* Weidenfeld & Nicolson, London, 1969

Mattingly, Harold *Imperial Roman Coinage* London, 1923

Roman Coins Methuen, London, 1955

Milne, J. G. *Greek and Roman Coins and the Study of History* Methuen, London, 1939

Newell, Edward T. *Royal Greek Portrait Coins* Whitman, Racine

Seaby, H. A. *Catalogue of Roman Coins* Seaby, London (various editions)

    Greek Coins and their Values Seaby, London, 1966
    Roman Silver Coins Seaby, London, 1952
Sear, D. R. *Roman Coins and their Values* Seaby, London, 1955
Seltman, Charles *Greek Coins* Methuen, London, 1955
    Masterpieces of Greek Coinage Bruno Cassirer, Oxford, 1949
    A Book of Greek Coins King Penguin, London, 1952
Stevenson, Seth *A Dictionary of Roman Coins* Seaby, London.

index

139

141